# Vietnam

## Contents

East Asia – 1945 to 1975


**4 VIETNAM, CAMBODIA & LAOS AT WAR 1945-1961**

The French, Chinese, Americans, Russians, Cambodians and Laotians all had a role to play in the fate of Vietnam in the post-World War Two era

**14 1962: *RANCH HAND* AND HELICOPTER GUNSHIPS**

The year that saw the US introduce a number of radical new forms of warfare in the Vietnam theatre – from chemical spraying to armed helicopters

**22 1963: THE RISE OF EAGLE FLIGHT**

Following a disastrous start, the ARVN and US advisers soon streamlined the helicopter born air assault process in 1963. However, the year was marred by political coups and the loss of a leader

**28 1964: JOHNSON DECLARES WAR ON THE NORTH**

In a year that saw seven changes of government in Vietnam and a new US President finding his feet, America widened the war against North Vietnam

**38 1965: SEARCHING FOR SAMs AND DOWNING MIGs**

The rules of engagement were relaxed and the war in Vietnam 'hotted up'

**48 1966: BIG BELLY BUFFS, CHINOOK GUNSHIPS AND *FISHBED* KILLERS**

The peak years of the war in South East Asia began in 1966 – from which point the US Armed Forces found themselves fighting not one war but three.

**54 1967: INTER-SERVICE RIVALRY AND A FALSE SENSE OF SECURITY**

In a year that saw the introduction of Sandy Skyraiders, Misty Super Sabres, Jolly Green Giants and Spectres, the US forces enjoyed a number of major successes

**62 1968: THE DEADLIEST YEAR**

In the year the US death toll reached its highest the decisive victory in the Tet Offensive was a turning point in the war – but not for the right reasons

**70 1969: WITHDRAWAL AND SECRET MISSIONS**

In a year that saw US troop strengths down to 474,000, the new President had no qualms about authorising secret strikes

**74 1970: TAKING THE FIGHT TO CAMBODIA**

Despite a shrinking force of aircraft and personnel, the US continued to take the fight to the enemy, and made a daring raid to rescue American prisoners

**78 1971: CUTTING OFF THE SUPPLY CHAIN**

Offensives to cut off supply routes cost the Allies dearly. And it soon became obvious that Hanoi had no intention of scaling back its offensive

**81 1972: SNATCHING DEFEAT FROM THE JAWS OF VICTORY**

With North Vietnamese massing at the border and ready to invade, there wasn't much the rapidly depleted US forces could do to fend them off. It was time to call in reinforcements

**90 1973: OPERATION *HOMECOMING***

With the peace agreement signed, work began to bring home the US troops, prisoners and hardware. But the war in Laos and Cambodia continued to rage

**92 1974: THE AGE OF AUSTERITY**

With the promised US aid package slashed, the South Vietnamese Air Force was forced to mothball aircraft, reducing its capability to defend itself from the North

**94 1975: EVACUATION**

With the North Vietnamese rapidly overrunning the South, the VNAF put up a brave fight; but it was soon time to evacuate the country

**98 COUNTING THE COST**

The war in Vietnam officially lasted 19 years, 5 months, 4 weeks and 1 day and is estimated to have resulted in the deaths of more than 3,880,000 people

Front Cover: Tyson V Rininger. All other images via the author unless stated


**Vietnam**

**Author** Phil Chinnery. **Editor** Stephen Bridgewater. **Sub Editor** Rebecca Gibbs. **Proof Reading** Jamie Ewan. **Design and Layout** Paul Silk.

**Publisher and Managing Director** Adrian Cox. **Executive Chairman** Richard Cox. **Commercial Director** Ann Saundry.

**Distribution** Seymour Distribution Ltd +44 (0)20 7429 4000. **Printing** Warners (Midlands) PLC, The Maltings, Manor Lane, Bourne, Lincs PE10 9PH.

**ISBN is 9781910415467**





**Published by** Key Publishing Ltd, PO Box 100, Stamford, Lincs PE19 1XQ.
Tel: +44 (0) 1780 755131. Fax: +44 (0) 1780 757261. Website: www.keypublishing.com

# THE EARLY YEARS

## The French, Chinese, Americans, Russians, Cambodians and Laotians all had a role to play in the fate of Vietnam in the post-World War Two era

At the height of the Vietnam War, television news programmes around the world often featured captured American pilots being paraded through the streets of Hanoi en route to the famous Hoa Lo prison – the so-called 'Hanoi Hilton'. However, had those same pilots been downed over North Vietnam two decades earlier they would have received an entirely different reception.

US involvement in Vietnam began as long ago as 1945, when American pilots flew combat missions against the Japanese who had occupied French Indochina during World War Two. Their B-24 Liberator bombers were being shot down over the same terrain that F-105 Thunderchiefs would be, two decades later.

In an attempt to recover downed US aircrews, agents of the Office of Strategic Services (OSS) were parachuted into the hills of Annam towards the end of the war, to train and arm local guerrilla bands. These guerrillas would help search for American pilots and attempt to cut rail lines used by the Japanese. They were led by a man known as Ho Chi Minh.

### Ho Chi Minh

Ho was a Marxist-Leninist who had formed the Indochinese Communist Party in 1930, but to the Vietnamese Nationalist groups (who were fighting to rid their country not only of the Japanese, but also the French), Ho appeared to have American backing and they turned to him as their leader.

As the war came to an end, the Japanese were disarmed and with the French colonial overseers weak and disorganised, a vacuum existed which Ho Chi Minh was quick to fill. Ho's American-trained guerrillas, known as the Viet Minh, marched into Hanoi and with a groundswell of popular support, formed the Provisional Government.

Emperor Bao Dai abdicated on August 30, 1945 and two days later Ho Chi Minh's Nationalist forces issued a declaration of independence establishing the Democratic Republic of Vietnam.

In October the OSS teams were withdrawn following the death of an officer who was shot at a Viet Minh roadblock. The officer, Major Peter Dewey, was the first American to die in the Vietnam War.

Within months, a well-armed French expeditionary corps of three full divisions had begun to arrive and the Viet Minh once again prepared for war.

The French were determined to regain control of their former colony, but when negotiations in Paris broke down in October 1946, Ho ordered his 60,000 Viet Minh troops into the countryside to prepare for a protracted guerrilla war.

Ho Chi Minh, the legendary North Vietnamese leader

Fighting broke out in December 1946 and by mid-1949 the situation had reached a stalemate, despite the presence of over 150,000 French troops. At this time China fell to Mao's communist army and the Viet Minh suddenly found itself with an ally on its northern border that was willing to train it and supply large quantities of arms and ammunition.

Meanwhile, in Europe many of the Eastern European countries had fallen under Soviet control. As such, the USA began to assist France to return to her pre-war status, and this support was also extended to French policy in Indochina where France proposed to give only limited autonomy to Vietnam, Laos and Cambodia.

### American assistance

As the guerrilla war gathered momentum, France had to commit ever increasing military resources to Indochina and on February 16, 1950 the French government formally requested American military and economic assistance to help defeat the Viet Minh. The Truman administration concluded that "the threat of Communist aggression in Indochina is only one phase of anticipated Communist plans to seize all of Southeast Asia" and permission to send both equipment and financial assistance was approved in May.

Later that summer the USA established a Military Assistance Advisory Group (MAAG) in Saigon and military advisers began to arrive to assist the French wherever possible. USAF advisers and engineers were used to help maintain American-supplied aircraft, of which over

By the spring of 1954 the French Air Force had 25 Grumman F8F Bearcats in Vietnam

French Douglas B-26 Invader bombers joined the Bearcats in 1954

Victorious Viet Minh troops move into Dien Bien Phu as a French C-47 burns in the background. Eleven thousand French troops were taken prisoner

500 were eventually delivered. These included Douglas C-47 transport aircraft and Grumman F8F Bearcat fighters, the latter taken from US Navy and Marine Air Reserve squadrons.

Nonetheless, towards the end of 1950 the Viet Minh – now well-armed by the Chinese – went on the offensive. In December US-supplied aircraft dropped napalm on Viet Minh troops for the first time.

## Air Department

In 1951 the French created the Vietnamese National Army including a small air component known as the Air Department of the Joint General Staff. A training centre was established at Nha Trang to teach Vietnamese personnel to both fly and support the aircraft and by the end of the year the 1st Air Observation Squadron (AOS) had been formed, flying the Morane-Saulnier MS.500 Criquet (the French-built derivative of the Fieseler Storch).

The Criquet was the standard equipment for most of the French observation squadrons in Indochina and soon the 1st AOS began operating within French units against the Viet Minh in southern Vietnam. The French Air Force (FAF) made little effort to develop a self-sufficient Vietnamese air unit and used the Vietnamese merely as replacements within their own squadrons.

Following the formation of a second Criquet squadron at Hue in 1952, a number of light transport aircraft were supplied, including Beechcraft C-45s and Republic Seabee amphibians. These aircraft were used to equip the 1st Liaison Squadron, based at Saigon's municipal airport at Tan Son Nhut, and used to shuttle personnel and supplies along the coast between Hue and Saigon.

The Vietnamese government requested additional aircraft to equip a combat unit, but the best that the French could offer was the Dassault MD 315 Flamant transport aircraft, albeit fitted with bomb racks.

> **"A vacuum existed which Ho Chi Minh was quick to fill"**

While the fledgling Air Department was struggling to establish itself, the war was going badly for the French. By the summer of 1953 the Viet Minh had crossed the border into Laos and set up a revolutionary Pathet Lao government in the capital Luang Prabang.

## Operation *Castor*

During the drive towards Laos, the Viet Minh had overrun the French garrison and airfield at Dien Bien Phu in Northwest Vietnam and it was here that the first decisive battle of the Vietnam War would be fought.

French commander General Henri Navarre decided to try to lure the Viet Minh to a set-piece battle where they could be annihilated by French airpower and massed artillery. To goad the elusive Viet Minh to attack, General Navarre planned to establish an impregnable fortress deep in enemy territory where it could threaten the Viet Minh lines of communications. Dien Bien Phu was chosen because of its location at the junction of three main supply routes and its proximity to the border with Laos, ten miles away.

Operation *Castor* began on November 20, 1953 when 800 men of the French 1st Colonial Paratroop Battalion jumped out of 64 Douglas C-47 Skytrains over the village of Dien Bien Phu. They landed among two companies of Viet Minh, which they soon destroyed, with the loss of 40 men. Before long, 10,000 men were dug in around Dien Bien Phu, which lies in a valley about 180 miles from Hanoi, the nearest French air base.

Navarre's plan was basically sound, but it underestimated the ability of the Viet Minh to supply and reinforce its men around Dien Bien Phu. It also overestimated the ability of the FAF to supply the base by air.

General Giap, the Viet Minh commander, encircled the base with 40,000 troops, outnumbering the reinforced 15,000 defenders by almost three to one. By the time the assault began, the Viet Minh had dragged 200 artillery pieces into positions by hand to surround the base. Within a few days, the runway was cratered and unusable and FAF aircraft attempting to drop supplies to the shrinking garrison had to brave a murderous corridor of anti-aircraft fire. Some 48 aircraft were shot down during the 56-day assault.

**The 25 Bearcats supplied by the French formed the VNAF's 1st Fighter Squadron and were the air force's first true combat aircraft. These were followed by 32 C-47 transports which were supplied under the Military Assistance Program (MAP) to equip the 1st Air Transport Group**

**In 1951 the French created the Vietnamese National Army including a small air component known as the Air Department of the Joint General Staff. The first aircraft to join it were Morane-Saulnier MS.500 Criquets - the French-built derivative of the Fieseler Storch**

> " French C-47s had to brave a murderous corridor of anti-aircraft fire "

Even at this early stage, the American Central Intelligence Agency (CIA) was involved in activities in both North and South Vietnam. In an effort to assist the beleaguered French, the CIA's covert airline Civil Air Transport (CAT) was contracted to fly in supplies using twin boom C-119 Flying Boxcar transports. These were provided by the USAF but flown by civilian crews.

During the closing stages of the battle, American reconnaissance aircraft overflew the area while American leaders discussed whether to intervene in the conflict. Even the use of tactical nuclear weapons against the hills surrounding Dien Bien Phu was considered. Ultimately, the President, no doubt influenced by the recently ended Korean War, decided that the risks of intervention outweighed the potential gains. The French were on their own.

On May 7, 1954, having suffered over 7,000 killed or wounded, the defenders of Dien Bien Phu surrendered to the Viet Minh (whose estimated casualties were over 20,000 including 8,000 killed). An estimated 11,000 French troops passed into captivity from which only half would return due to lack of proper medical care, harsh conditions and inadequate food.

## 17th Parallel

The defeat of the French army at Dien Bien Phu marked the beginning of the end of French influence in Indochina. The very next day at a previously scheduled international conference in Geneva, Switzerland, representatives of the major powers and of the Indochinese people met to discuss a ceasefire agreement, which was subsequently approved on July 20/21.

The outcome of the agreement was that Vietnam would be divided along the 17th Parallel into a communist North and a non-communist South; there would be a five-mile demilitarised zone (DMZ) on either side of the border; French and Viet Minh forces would withdraw north and south of the DMZ and in two years elections would be held to decide the issue of reunification of the whole country.

The division of the country led to the establishment of two rival governments in Hanoi in the North and Saigon in the South.

Bao Dai had appointed Ngo Dinh Diem as Premier in the South in June 1954, and he set about creating separate armed forces. As a result, the Vietnamese Air Force (VNAF) came into existence on July 1, 1955 – although at this time it existed more in name than in reality.

When Dien Bien Phu fell to the Viet Minh, South Vietnam had only 58 aircraft and approximately 1,345 aviation personnel. As the French began to withdraw their forces, it replaced the VNAF's Criquets with Cessna O-1 Bird

In March 1958 the first Sikorsky H-19 helicopters arrived for the Vietnamese Air Department and were formed into the 1st Helicopter Squadron. This is a USAF example.

Dogs and the Flamants with 25 Grumman Bearcats – the latter forming the 1st Fighter Squadron. These were followed by 32 C-47 transports, which were supplied under the USA's Military Assistance Program (MAP) to equip the 1st Air Transport Group.

The USA decided to expand its influence in Indochina to try to contain the spread of communism and in February 1955 the Senate ratified the creation of the South East Asia Treaty Organisation (SEATO), whose eight members guaranteed the protection of Laos, Cambodia and 'the free territory under the jurisdiction of the State of Vietnam'.

Following a decision that the USA would provide aid directly to South Vietnam rather than through France, MAAG began to assume responsibility for training the South Vietnamese Army. On November 1, 1955, America officially joined what would become known as the Vietnam War.

Meanwhile, the French would continue to train the VNAF until May 1957 when American advisers took over. Some Vietnamese cadets were trained 'in country' on North American T-6 Texans, while others were sent to Clark AFB in the Philippines or to the USA for more advanced training. More equipment began to arrive under MAP, including enough C-47s to form a second Transport Group. In March 1958 the first Sikorsky H-19 helicopters arrived and were formed into the 1st Helicopter Squadron.

Although it was now a functioning air force, the VNAF was ill equipped to deal with any threat posed by its communist neighbour in the North.

## Elections

In October 1955, President Diem organised an election within South Vietnam to decide whether the country should continue as a monarchy headed by Bao Dai, or as a Republic led by himself. The referendum was organised by Diem's brother Ngo Dinh Nhu and resulted in an unconvincing 99% vote in favour of the Republic.

The nationwide elections due to be held in July 1956 would never take place. South Vietnam had not been party to the French-Viet Minh agreement and argued that the northerners would not be able to vote freely under Ho Chi Minh's one-party rule and that the block vote of the North would overwhelm those cast in the South.

Of course, the true reason for Diem's refusal may have been that although Ho Chi Minh was a communist, he was a legendary hero to the Vietnamese people and would probably have won any nationwide election.

Meanwhile, Ho had taken out insurance against the failure of the reunification elections to take place. During the ten months following the signing of the Geneva Agreement, approximately 900,000 Vietnamese had resettled in the South, while 90,000 Viet Minh returned to the North. However, Ho had ordered 10,000 of his communist supporters to go to ground in South Vietnam and had buried enough arms to field 6,000 guerrillas if the need arose.

**When Dien Bien Phu fell to the Viet Minh, South Vietnam had only 58 aircraft and approximately 1,345 aviation personnel. Later, 32 C-47 transports were supplied under the USA's Military Assistance Program (MAP) to equip the 1st Air Transport Group** *(USAF Museum)*

**International delegates at the 1954 Geneva conference discuss the agreement that would see Vietnam divided along the 17th Parallel into a communist North and a non-communist South** *(USAF Museum)*

**The CIA began to recruit an army of Meo tribesmen, led by a Meo chief named Vang Pao who had fought for the French against the Viet Minh. This photo was taken at Lima Site 20A and shows Vang Pao's men training for a summer push north from the Plain of Jars**

By the end of 1957, insurgent forces in the south, known by the derogatory name of Viet Cong (Vietnamese Communist) had begun to carry out terrorist acts against Diem's regime.

By May 1959 it had become obvious to the leaders in the North that their attempt to reunify the country through a nationwide election had failed and they announced that the country would be reunified by an armed struggle instead. Two months later, a US Army major and master sergeant were killed during a Viet Cong attack on Bien Hoa Air Base (AB) and in September several Viet Cong companies ambushed a force of Army of the Republic of Vietnam (ARVN) troops on the marshy Plain of Reeds southwest of Saigon. According to the Viet Cong, this incident marked the official start of the armed struggle.

Supported by the North and aided by Diem's increasingly repressive rule, the strength of the Viet Cong grew and in October, American officials asked for an increase in the strength of the MAAG from 342 men to 685, so as to provide more US Army Special Forces teams to train ARVN Rangers for border patrols. Despite communist protests to the International Control Commission (ICC), the request was approved and the additional Green Berets began to arrive.

## Ho Chi Minh Trail

Towards the end of 1959 a North Vietnamese Army (NVA) transportation group began work on the Ho Chi Minh Trail; an infiltration route of tracks and roads running north to south along the Annamite Mountains into Laos and Cambodia and fanning out into the jungles of South Vietnam.

Soon the first of an initial 4,500-man military cadre began to arrive in South Vietnam. They were mostly ethnic southerners who had received indoctrination and training in the north. These hardcore Viet Cong were funnelled into communist jungle base areas in Tay Ninh Province on the Cambodian border (later designated War Zone C by American officials); an area northwest of Saigon known as War Zone D and also into the dense U Minh forest area of the Ca Mau peninsula.

In the meantime, the USA had not been idle. Major airfield construction efforts had commenced at Ubon, Udorn and Chiang Mai in Thailand and new runways had been planned for the airfields at Vientiane and Tan Son Nhut.

By the summer of 1960, the VNAF was experiencing problems with its obsolete equipment and all of the Bearcats had been grounded due to structural deficiencies. The USA responded by shipping the first of 25 former US Navy Douglas A-1 Skyraiders and the first eleven Sikorsky H-34 Choctaw helicopters. Unfortunately, spares and servicing problems kept many of the Skyraiders and H-34s on the ground.

North Vietnam recognised the strategic importance of Laos as a relatively safe infiltration route around the DMZ and into South Vietnam. After the Geneva Conference in 1954 (which conferred independence on the kingdoms of Laos and Cambodia, as well as signalling the end of French rule in Vietnam), around 7,000 Viet Minh remained illegally in Laos and these formed the backbone of the communist Pathet Lao guerrilla movement.

**The USA shipped 25 former US Navy Douglas A-1 Skyraider aircraft to Vietnam in September 1960 to replace the ageing F8F Bearcats. Lack of spare parts and servicing problems kept many of the aircraft on the ground**

**In order to supply and provide transport for such a large force, the CIA's covert airline, Air America, assembled a huge fleet of aircraft, including STOL types, such as this Helio-Courier, seen in neighbouring Laos** *(USAF Museum)*

**An Air America C-46 Commando wearing a US civil registration number. Many of the transport types were provided direct from US military stocks and most were flown either unmarked or wearing false markings**

By 1957 the Pathet Lao had won control over the mountain town of Tchepone from the Royal Lao Army. The town was the key crossroads of a trail network leading into South Vietnam's Central Highlands and the Mekong Delta, the 'rice bowl' of Vietnam.

American was forbidden by the Geneva Agreement to establish a large military advisory mission in Laos, so in 1958 a Program Evaluation Office (PEO) was established instead.

The PEO was in fact a CIA cover for a whole range of clandestine activities against the Pathet Lao and their North Vietnamese sponsors.

## Air America

Within a year the Special Forces 'White Star' teams and CIA officers had organised over 9,000 Meo guerrillas, and soon they were blowing up communist supply dumps and harassing their logistics lines. Eventually, the Meo army expanded to over 40,000 guerrillas and became the most effective irregular fighting force in Laos.

In order to supply and provide transport for such a large force, the CIA's covert airline, Air America, assembled a huge fleet of aircraft, including short take-off and landing (STOL) types such as the Helio-Courier, PC-6 Pilatus Porter and Dornier Do-28, and transport aircraft like the C-7 Caribou, C-46 Commando, C-47 Skytrain and C-123 Provider. Many of the transport types were provided direct from US military stocks and most were flown unmarked or wearing false markings.

The situation in Laos was further complicated by the traditional pattern of competition among a few ruling families and by 1960 a three-way civil war was underway between rightists, neutralists and the Pathet Lao. Events came to a head on August 9 when Captain Kong Le, a paratrooper battalion commander, disgusted with the continuing civil war, used the opportunity of a royal funeral to take control of Vientiane, dissolve the right-wing cabinet of Prince Somsanith and invite Prince Souvanna Phouma to form a neutralist Laotian government.

When news of the coup reached General Phoumi Nosavan, a right-wing military leader who dominated the Sannikone government, flew to his home in Savannakhet and from there he established a 'Committee Against the Coup d'Etat' alongside most of the conservatives in the National Assembly.

The US government began backing the 'Savannakhet' group with money and arms (while maintaining formal diplomatic relations with Phouma's Vientiane government) but in late November, Nosavan's troops marched on Vientiane. A battle raged around the city for three days before Kong Le retreated northwards to the Plain of Jars with the remnants of his followers.

## First USAF loss

In early December, Kong Le and North Vietnamese Army units operating in northeast Laos, began receiving arms and supplies from a Soviet airlift.

On December 16 the American Air Attaché, Col Butler B Toland Jr, photographed a Soviet Ilyushin Il-14 *Crate* dropping supplies to the Kong Le forces near Vang Vieng and a few days later the

USAF airmen train South Vietnamese pilots how to fly and fight the North American T-28 Trojan at Bien Hoa Air Base in 1961 *(USAF Museum)*

USAF advisers asked for a detachment of RF-101 Voodoos to deploy to Tan Son Nhut to conduct reconnaissance missions over Vietnam and Laos – and, cleverly, an invitation from the VNAF for the USAF to take part in an airshow provided the excuse to send RF-101 Voodoos from the 15th TRS to Saigon in 1961. In 31 days they flew 67 sorties over the Laotian Plain of Jars and parts of the Ho Chi Minh Trail until they were withdrawn following North Vietnamese complaints to the ICC *(USAF Museum)*

US Embassy's VC-47 Skytrain was on a reconnaissance flight over the Plain of Jars when it was fired upon by Kong Le and Pathet Lao troops. This was the first USAF aircraft fired at by the communists in the Southeast Asia conflict and a 0.50-calibre machine gun bullet wounded the radio operator.

In March 1961, President John F Kennedy announced to a press conference that the Russians had flown over 1,000 supply flights into Laos.

A few days later, on March 23, the first American aircraft was lost to enemy action. A specially modified intelligence gathering SC-47 took off from Vientiane and set a course for a Pathet Lao base on the eastern edge of the Plain of Jars, called Xieng Khouangville. The SC-47's mission was to determine the frequencies used by Soviet pilots to locate the airfield through the dense fog that often covered the area. Suddenly, shells from a Pathet Lao anti-aircraft gun slammed into the aircraft, shearing off a wing and sending the plane plummeting towards the jungle. A US Army major who habitually wore a parachute jumped from the falling aircraft and was captured by the Pathet Lao. He spent 17 months as a prisoner before being repatriated.

## Covert support

President Kennedy did not want to commit American ground troops to combat in Laos, but was prepared to support the pro-Western forces by covert means. Air America received 16 H-34 Choctaw helicopters and these were flown in Laos by civilian crews.

In addition, the survival of the neutralist government depended on the acquisition of useful intelligence about enemy activities, so the US secretly sent reconnaissance and combat aircraft to Thailand.

The Royal Thai Air Force had been providing reconnaissance support to Laos with their Lockheed RT-33A Shooting Star jets, but in February 1961 they were withdrawn. President Kennedy was reluctant to authorise use of USAF McDonnell RF-101 Voodoo jets, so some RT-33s were borrowed from the Philippine Air Force, painted with Laotian markings and flown on reconnaissance missions over Laos by Air Force pilots.

The first of these sorties was flown on April 24, 1961 under the code name *Field Goal*. Eight days earlier, six North American F-100 Super Sabre fighters from the 510th Tactical Fighter Squadron (TFS) at Clark AFB in the Philippines had flown into Don Muang International Airport outside Bangkok, ostensibly to provide air defence, under the code name *Bell Tone*.

The USA and USSR realised that their two countries were on a possible collision course in Laos and arranged an

Ngo Dinh Diem was appointed as South Vietnam's Premier in June 1954

In 1961 the USA agreed to increase its military aid to South Vietnam by funding a second fighter squadron. The unit was to be made up of North American T-28 Trojans, taken out of storage in America and modified as T-28Ds. It was felt that because of its robust construction and ability to withstand hard landings, the T-28 would be very suitable in the counter-insurgency role *(USAF Museum)*

international conference to work out a political solution to the Laotian problem. The Geneva Conference on Laos opened in May 1961, and lasted until July 1962 when the three Lao factions (Neutralists, Pathet Lao and Rightists) finally agreed on a delicate settlement. Prince Souvanna Phouma established a coalition, which lasted until fighting resumed in April 1963.

The 1962 Geneva Agreement stipulated a deadline for the withdrawal of all foreign military elements. Inspectors from the ICC checked and counted each military adviser as he left the country. There were 666 of them and by the deadline, the only uniformed Americans or intelligence officers left in Laos were the Army and Air Force attachés and their staffs at the Embassy. The ICC could not check the communist foreign military out of the country, as they were not permitted to visit Pathet Lao territory. It was estimated that there were 10,000 regular soldiers from North Vietnam still in the country. Behind this phony neutrality, which existed only in the world's newspapers and in diplomats' minds, the war continued.

In fact, as early as 1960 the Central Committee of the Lao Dong Party (the Communist party of North Vietnam), had passed a resolution that South Vietnam was to be 'liberated' and that North and South Vietnam were to be unified under a 'progressive socialist' administration. In December, Hanoi Radio announced the formation in South Vietnam of the National Front for the Liberation of South Vietnam, which it claimed was made up of several South Vietnamese political parties.

Subsequent broadcasts identified a 'People's Revolutionary Party' as the leading party in this so-called front. It is significant that no announcement of this came out of South Vietnam and no nationally-known South Vietnamese figure was ever identified with any of the political parties, which seemed to exist on paper only and in broadcasts by Hanoi radio.

The Viet Cong intensified its guerrilla war against President Ngo Dinh Diem's regime early in 1961. By March, US intelligence analysts estimated that the guerrillas were killing, assassinating or kidnapping 500 pro-government village officials, teachers and soldiers every month.

> “ Diem requested a treaty committing the USA to defend South Vietnam ”

## Presidential delegation

In May 1961, President Kennedy sent Vice-President Lyndon B Johnson to South Vietnam to consult with President Diem. As a result of the discussions, the USA agreed to increase its military aid by funding the expansion of the South Vietnamese Army from 170,000 to 200,000 men and providing the VNAF with a second fighter squadron. The squadron was to be made up of North American T-28 Trojans, taken out of storage in America and modified as T-28Ds. It was felt that because of its robust construction and ability to withstand hard landings, the T-28 would be very suitable in the counter-insurgency role.

A third liaison squadron equipped with O-1 Bird Dogs would be formed and eventually a photographic reconnaissance unit would also be provided. Additional training centres would be set up, including an American/South Vietnamese combat development and test centre which would improve counter-insurgency techniques and tactics. One of its ideas soon to be put into practice was the use of aerial-delivered defoliants to reduce jungle cover along major highways, where the Viet Cong frequently ambushed government convoys.

At this time the US armed forces had little knowledge or experience in the art of counter-insurgency warfare and Kennedy ordered that new units be formed to deal with this type of conflict. The USAF responded by establishing the 4400th Combat Crew Training Squadron (CCTS) – codenamed *Jungle Jim* – at Eglin AFB in Florida on April 14, 1961.

In September 1961, Viet Cong attacks increased sharply and there were indications of some weakening in Diem's military position. At the end of the month Diem requested a treaty that would commit the USA to defend South Vietnam.

In response, President Kennedy sent his chief military adviser Gen Maxwell D Taylor to survey the situation. The news was not too good. It was Gen Taylor's view that South Vietnam was in trouble and major US interests were at stake. He argued that the communist strategy of taking over Southeast Asia by guerrilla warfare was well on its way to success in South Vietnam, aided by Diem's unpopular and inefficient government. Consequently, Kennedy approved a more active programme of support including additional deployments of Army aviation and USAF units.

## Farm Gate

On November 10, 1961 Detachment 2A of the 4,400th CCTS, designated *Farm Gate*, left Eglin for Vietnam. They took with them four SC-47 Skytrains, eight T-28s and four Douglas B-26 bombers (although the latter were listed as RB-26 reconnaissance

**Sixteen H-34 Choctaw helicopters were provided to Air America and these were flown by civilian crews** *(Jon Pote via Phil Chinnery)*

**In the summer of 1961 President Kennedy agreed to equip the Vietnamese Air Force with a third squadron of Cessna O-1 Bird Dog observation aircraft**

**In order to increase the number of operational T-28s, 30 US pilots were assigned to the two VNAF C-47 squadrons, thus releasing the Vietnamese C-47 pilots for attack assignments. The US pilots, nicknamed the 'Dirty Thirty', served as co-pilots with the Vietnamese crews until the unit disbanded in December 1963** *(USAF Museum)*

aircraft, rather than bombers to stay in line with the Geneva Agreement which forbade the introduction of bombers into Indochina). Significantly, all the aircraft carried Vietnamese Air Force markings.

One of the detachment's first tasks was to get the Vietnamese's existing T-28s operational and after extensive instruction in gunnery and bombing, this was achieved by March 1962.

In order to increase the number of operational T-28s, 30 US pilots were assigned to the two VNAF C-47 squadrons, thus releasing the Vietnamese C-47 pilots for attack assignments. The US pilots, nicknamed the 'Dirty Thirty', served as co-pilots with the Vietnamese crews until the unit disbanded in December 1963.

Towards the end of 1961, communist Pathet Lao forces accelerated their operations against the Royal Government of Laos. At the same time, several Viet Cong units of up to 1,500 men began attacking strategic highways in the vicinity of Saigon and other urban areas, leading President Diem to declare a state of emergency.

## Voodoos 'on show'

USAF advisers asked for a detachment of RF-101 Voodoos to deploy to Tan Son Nhut to conduct reconnaissance missions over Vietnam and Laos – and, cleverly, an invitation from the VNAF for the USAF to take part in an airshow provided the excuse to send jets into the area. On October 18, four RF-101Cs from the 15th Tactical Reconnaissance Squadron (TRS) deployed to Saigon under the codename *Pipe Stem*.

Over the following 31 days they flew 67 sorties over the Laotian Plain of Jars and parts of the Ho Chi Minh Trail until they were withdrawn following North Vietnamese complaints to the ICC.

In order to replace the Tan Son Nhut detachment, the Royal Thai government agreed to let USAF RF-101s operate out of Don Muang airport and on November 7, the Able Mabel task force became operational when four RF-101Cs of the 45th TRS arrived from Japan. By the end of the year they had flown 130 missions.

One of the problem areas highlighted by Gen Taylor was the inadequate road networks and geographical conditions that often hindered the movement of Army of the Republic of the Vietnam (ARVN) troops by vehicle. Neither were there enough helicopters to go around. President Kennedy therefore decided to send a USAF squadron of 16 Fairchild C-123B Provider tactical assault transport aircraft under the codename *Mule Train*, and these began to arrive at Tan Son Nhut in December.

At the same time, Kennedy also ordered the deployment of US Army helicopter units to Vietnam and on December 11 the USS *Card* sailed into Saigon with the Piasecki CH-21C Shawnees of the 8th and 57th Transportation Companies (Light Helicopter) on board. The Shawnee, nicknamed the 'Flying Banana' was a single-engined twin-rotor helicopter, which was underpowered and slow. But under the circumstances anything was better than nothing and soon the helicopters were on their way to Tan Son Nhut airport where they were prepared for operations as the first major American unit in Vietnam.

The war was intensifying…

Two C-123 *Ranch Hand* aircraft from the 309th Air Commando Squadron. *Ranch Hand* C-123s began spraying operations in September 1962 and over the next ten years over 19 million gallons of herbicides would be sprayed over South Vietnam *(USAF Museum)*

# *RANCH HAND* AND HELICOPTER GUNSHIPS

**The new year saw the US introduce a number of radical new forms of warfare in the Vietnam theatre – from chemical spraying to armed helicopters**

The USAF's priority in early 1962 was to assist the Vietnamese in setting up a Tactical Air Control System (TACS), which was essential to the proper employment of airpower within the theatre.

Although the VNAF was nominally responsible for the system, the USAF in fact operated the TACS from the outset and a Control and Reporting Centre (CRC) – the main part of the system with the heaviest radars – was installed at Tan Son Nhut AB. A Control and Reporting Post (CRP) was then established at Da Nang, followed by a Vietnamese-operated radar CRP at Pleiku.

This radar network provided limited aircraft control and warning coverage over all of South Vietnam and soon began picking up tracks of numerous unidentified aircraft.

In normal day-to-day operation, the TACS was concerned mainly with the control of aircraft and ensuring that they carry out their assigned missions. Meanwhile, the air-ground operations system is the heart of the decision making process in determining what, where and when those aircraft will strike. It is the air-ground operations system that can make or break close air support effectiveness.

Prior to the US involvement in the process, there was only a very rudimentary air-ground operations system between the ARVN and VNAF and no overall commander of combat operations.

The four Corps Commanders operated almost autonomously, with I Corps covering the northern part of the country adjacent to the DMZ; II Corps the Central Highlands; III Corps the area surrounding Saigon and IV Corps the southern delta.

When American aircraft started being introduced to the theatre of operations, a change in the slow and inadequate system was needed to conform with accepted USAF doctrine. As such, Air Support Operations Centres (ASOCs) – later re-designated Direct Air Support Centres (DASCs) – were established at each of the Corps headquarters and manned by both VNAF and USAF personnel.

## Operation *Chopper*

The deployment of the TACS began on January 1, 1962 under the codename *Barn Door*, and the newly-arrived H-21 Shawnee helicopters prepared to go into action. Within a fortnight of arriving in Vietnam, the 8th and 57th Transportation Companies carried out Operation *Chopper*, the first major airlift of the war.

Over 1,000 ARVN paratroopers and their American advisers were airlifted into a Viet Cong base complex a mere 10 miles west of Saigon. The Viet Cong were surprised by this first large-scale use of helicopters and offered little resistance, melting away into the surrounding jungle and leaving behind a quantity of supplies and a transmitter which had been used to broadcast anti-government propaganda. A number of problems had shown up during the operation though, including poor air-ground communications and embarkation/disembarkation difficulties experienced by the relatively small ARVN troops who found it hard to climb aboard and jump out of the helicopters with full packs and equipment.

Soon the H-21 companies found themselves extremely overworked and, in January 1962, the 93rd Transportation Company was sent on board the USS *Card* to join them.

Although there were now three helicopter companies in the country (two at Tan Son Nhut and one at Da Nang), a critical shortage of engines and deterioration of rotor blades and other equipment due to the high humidity caused huge problems. In order to establish a utility supply network for the H-21s, the 18th Aviation Company was sent out from Fort Riley, Kansas, with their U-1A Otter aircraft and were soon flying parts and supplies the length and breadth of the country.

Shortly thereafter two more light helicopter companies, the 33rd and 81st, were deployed and the five H-21 units deployed throughout the four military regions into which South Vietnam had been divided.

## Operation *Ranch Hand*

At 16.30 on January 7, 1962, three Fairchild C-123 Providers landed at Tan Son Nhut AB and taxied to a secure fenced area. They had come from Clark AFB in the

Tan Son Nhut air base was also Saigon's civil airport and a Pan Am Boeing 707 and C-141 Starlifter can be seen here behind the squadrons of VNAF C-47s *(USAF Museum)*

Philippines where they and three other such transport aircraft had spent the previous month waiting for Presidential clearance to proceed to Vietnam.

These were no ordinary Providers, for they had aluminium alloy armour plating under and around the cockpit and were fitted with the MC-1 Hourglass spray system complete with 1000US Gal spray tank and under-wing nozzles.

They had arrived to begin Operation *Ranch Hand*. The idea had originated at the Combat Development and Test Centre and had four objectives; first of which was to strip the Cambodian-Laotian-North Vietnamese border of foliage to remove the protective cover from Viet Cong reinforcements. Secondly, it was to defoliate a portion of the Mekong Delta area known as War Zone D, in which the Viet Cong had many bases and thirdly it was to destroy numerous abandoned mangroves that the Viet Cong used as food sources. Finally, Operation *Ranch Hand* was to destroy mangrove swamps within which the Viet Cong took refuge – but unfortunately the programme would have meant the defoliation of over 31,000 square miles of jungle, an area equivalent to about half of South Vietnam. This ambitious plan was soon dropped in favour of a more limited scheme.

By then the USAF had flown some 35,000lbs of herbicides into Vietnam, bypassing ICC inspection. Soon afterwards, the US Department of Defense announced that in view of the acts of aggression being carried out by North Vietnam, in flagrant violation of the Geneva Accords, the USA would no longer announce the arrival of personnel and equipment to the ICC. During early January 1962, more than 200,000US Gal of chemicals were aboard two cargo ships: destination Vietnam.

The first *Ranch Hand* test flights took place on January 10, 1962 and formal operations commenced three days later. Flown by USAF pilots, a Vietnamese 'aircraft commander' flew alongside him to give the impression that it was a Vietnamese operation but had no actual authority over the mission. In fact, on one occasion when an American pilot persuaded his Vietnamese 'aircraft commander' to take over the controls, his erratic handling soon convinced the crew that he was not a pilot. It was subsequently learned that the VNAF had been sending navigators instead of pilots and, later, would merely send anyone who happened to be available, whether officer or enlisted!

The defoliation operations were not without cost however, because on February 2 a *Ranch Hand* C-123 crashed, killing the crew of three.

Shortly afterwards, the 13th Air Force, which had recently established a detachment at Tan Son Nhut, requested fighter escorts for all future *Ranch Hand* operations. Nine days later the first *Farm Gate* [see introduction] aircraft was lost when an SC-47A on a leaflet dropping mission crashed in the mountains 70 miles

Vietnamese airborne rangers, their two US advisers, and a team of 12 US Special Forces troops set out to raid a Viet Cong supply base 62 miles northwest of Saigon as their Piasecki H-21 Shawnee helicopter departs for base *(USAF Museum)*

**A pair of USAF C-123 Providers fly over the mainland USA in the 1950s. The type would go on to serve an important, if controversial role in the Vietnam War** *(USAF Museum)*

**▲ In order to establish a utility supply network for the H-21 helicopters, the 18th Aviation Company was sent out from Fort Riley, Kansas, with their U-1A Otter aircraft and these were soon flying parts and supplies the length and breadth of the country**

**► An alleged Viet Cong activist, captured during an attack on an American outpost near the Cambodian border, is interrogated** *(USAF Museum)*

northeast of Saigon. Secretary of Defense McNamara subsequently criticised the mission and re-emphasised that American forces were supposed to be training the Vietnamese, not undertaking combat activities.

## Agent Orange

The defoliation flights continued until March 20, when they were suspended for five months for the programme to be re-evaluated. Villagers complained of damage to their trees and crops by the defoliant, which often spread over a greater area than planned, and this was soon used to full advantage by Viet Cong propagandists.

*Ranch Hand* C-123s resumed spraying operations in September 1962 and over the next ten years over 19 million gallons of herbicides would be sprayed over South Vietnam. Eleven million gallons were of the type known as Agent Orange (as identified by the coloured bands around the drums), which consisted of a mixture of dichlorophen-oxyacetic and tricholorphen-oxyacetic acids.

The defoliation programme was halted in 1971, following the banning of the chemicals in the USA due to their possible effects on humans. By the end of the programme 41% of the mangrove forests in South Vietnam had been affected, together with 19% of the uplands forests and 8% of all cultivated land. Despite the best intentions of the USAF, Agent Orange was sprayed not only over the countryside, but over the soldiers and civilian population as well. At the time of writing over 16,000 veterans had filed disability claims against the US Government for health damage allegedly due to Agent Orange.

## Forward Air Control

On January 13, 1962, (the same day the *Ranch Hand* missions began), T-28 Trojans from the 4400th CCTS's *Farm Gate* detachment flew their first Forward Air Controller (FAC)-directed mission against Viet Cong who were besieging an ARVN outpost. The Forward Air Controllers in their Cessna O-1 Bird Dogs and the Air Liaison Officers on the ground were the last elements in the air-ground operations system. The FAC would ensure that the ground-attack aircraft delivered their ordnance in the right place, usually marking the target area with rockets mounted under their wings.

Although the *Farm Gate* aircraft were officially there in the combat training role, they were authorised to fire back if fired upon. This was then extended to undertaking actual combat operations, but only when a VNAF crewman was aboard or when the VNAF lacked the ability to perform certain missions.

In January alone, *Farm Gate* T-28s and B-26 Invader bombers attacked targets from Saigon to as far north as Quang Tri Province, near the DMZ in 229 combat sorties. The SC-47s also performed various leaflet drops, psychological warfare broadcasts and Night Angel flare-drop missions – the latter were the salvation of many outposts and strategic hamlets in the strife-torn countryside. Usually the Viet Cong would attack under the cover of darkness, especially just

Operation *Ranch Hand* was to destroy mangrove swamps and foliage where the Viet Cong took refuge or obtained their food. *(USAF Museum)*

Defoliation sorties were also conducted by helicopters such as this UH-1 Iroquois *(USAF Museum)*

509th Fighter-Interceptor Squadron F-102s on the flightline at Tan Son Nhut Air Base in March 1962. The aircraft had been sent from Clark AFB in the Philippines on Temporary Duty (TDY) to provide air defence of Saigon *(USAF Museum)*

before daylight. To counter this, 'flare-ships' would fly an all-night vigil over certain portions of the country, ready to heed the call of a besieged outpost. Often the brilliant illumination produced by the paraflares would be enough to cause the Viet Cong to break off their attack, fearing the arrival of a subsequent airstrike.

The VNAF began to increase its number of sorties by flying both day and night and in January its single squadron of 22 Douglas A-1H Skyraiders flew 251 sorties.

Ironically, it was VNAF Skyraiders that gave the Tactical Air Control System its first operational test when two disaffected VNAF pilots strafed and bombed the presidential palace in Saigon on February 27, 1962. One aircraft was shot down while the other escaped to Cambodia.

One area in which the VNAF began to prove its mettle was in convoy and train escort, and losses from Viet Cong ambushes declined sharply when the VNAF began to put an O-1 Bird Dog FAC and a flight of strike aircraft above each important convoy. A similar result was achieved when strike aircraft began escorting both passenger and freight trains along portions of the railroad where communist attacks were most frequent. Whereas escort missions between January and July 1962 totalled slightly over 100, by the autumn that figure had reached nearly 200 per month.

> "The VNAF had been sending navigators instead of pilots"

Unidentified radar tracks over South Vietnam on March 19 and 20, 1962 prompted the Commander-in-Chief Pacific (CINCPAC) to direct the deployment of four Convair F-102 Delta Dagger interceptors* to Tan Son Nhut a day later. The first Operation *Water Glass* (later '*Candy Machine*') sorties and were flown by three F-102As and one TF-102A from the 509th Fighter Interceptor Squadron (FIS) but one week later they returned to Clark AFB without making any active intercepts. Additional *Water Glass* deployments continued throughout the year, using two-seat TF-102As, which were more effective against the low-slow targets.

## Marine Corps

With the USAF and US Army already having operational squadrons in Vietnam, it was the turn of the US Marine Corps (USMC) to join the war in March 1962 when it was ordered to deploy a helicopter squadron to the region and planning began for Operation *Shufly*.

On April 9, Col John F Carey, the Chief of Staff of the 1st Marine Air Wing, and his staff arrived at Soc Trang; an airfield some 85 miles southwest of Saigon in the Mekong Delta. It had been built by the Japanese during World War Two and had a 3,000ft long concrete runway, a distinct bonus in the Delta where most roads and runways were surfaced with laterite, a red clay which has the consistency of talcum powder when dry, and glue when wet.

Four *Ranch Hand* C-123 Providers spray liquid defoliant on a suspected Viet Cong position in South Vietnam. The four specially equipped aircraft covered a 1,000ft wide swath in each pass over the dense vegetation *(USAF Museum)*

On April 15, Marine Helicopter Squadron HMM-362 flew its 24 Sikorsky UH-34D Seahorses off the USS Princeton and into Soc Trang. They were accompanied by a C-117 for transport and liaison and three O-1B Bird Dogs from Marine Squadron VMO-2

A UTTHCO UH-1A undergoing tests. A single machine gun was fitted to each landing skid and fed from ammunition boxes inside the cargo compartment, while eight launch tubes for the rockets were fixed to the rear of each skid. Three platoons of UH-1As arrived at Tan Son Nhut Air Base on July 25 and flew their first escort mission for the H-21s nine days later

“The Viet Cong were surprised by this large-scale use of helicopters”

Other airfield facilities were non-existent, however, so the Douglas C-117 that ferried Carey to the region was converted into an improvised control tower to give landing instructions to the KC-130 Hercules transports bringing fuel, water and supplies into the airfield. Six days later, Marine Helicopter Squadron HMM-362 flew its 24 Sikorsky UH-34D Seahorses off the USS *Princeton* into Soc Trang. The helicopters were accompanied by a further C-117 (for transport and liaison) and three Cessna O-1B Bird Dogs from Marine Squadron VMO-2.

Within ten days one of the H-34s had been shot down by a single bullet, which pierced an oil pipe in the engine and highlighted the need for armour plating around such vulnerable areas. The squadron swapped bases with the 93rd Aviation Company at Da Nang in June, mainly because the H-34s were more capable of operating in the high elevations of the northern portion of the country than the underpowered H-21's, which were also only marginally suited for night and instrument flying.

By the time HMM-362 was relieved in August, it had identified almost every weakness in the early helicopters. Armour plating was needed, as was some form of firepower to help suppress enemy ground fire. New body armour and flight clothing for crews was given a high priority. Also urgently needed was an armed escort for the troop-carrying helicopters, to immediately attack any enemy around the landing zone. In this particular field, the US Army was way ahead.

## Armed 'Hueys'

The Army's H-21 helicopters had started to receive ground fire when flying into and out of landing zones. The crew chiefs initially responded by returning fire with infantry weapons and later mounted 0.30in Browning machine guns in the open doorways. Even if the disadvantage of partially blocking the doorways was discounted, this suppressive fire was not enough and fixed-wing aircraft were not always available for escort duties. It soon became evident that the solution to the problem might be in the employment of armed gunship helicopters.

The 53rd Aviation Detachment had been operating 15 Bell UH-1A Iroquois as part of the Aviation Support Activity on the island of Okinawa and in July 1962 these 'Hueys' (from the original designation HU-

It would be in Vietnam that the helicopter really proved its worth as a weapon of war

A gunship engages a target in the Mekong Delta. The co-pilot on the left fires the machine guns and aims with the sight mounted on the cabin roof, while the pilot on the right fires the rockets by aiming the helicopter at the target

The UH-1B gunship improved in leaps and bounds. Bill McGee's gunship has twin machine guns and eight rockets mounted alongside the fuselage. In this photo the guns have been removed for cleaning

1A) were used to form the Utility Tactical Transport Helicopter Company (UTTHCO).

Under the guidance of Warrant Officer Cletus Heck, the Hueys were fitted with a locally fabricated weapons system consisting of two fixed forward-firing 0.30in machine guns and 16 2.75in folding-fin aerial rockets procured from the Air Force. A single machine gun was fitted to each landing skid and fed from ammunition boxes inside the cargo compartment, while eight launch tubes for the rockets were fixed to the rear of each skid.

The three platoons of UH-1As arrived at Tan Son Nhut Air Base on July 25 and flew their first escort mission for the H-21s nine days later. The suppressive fire delivered by the armed helicopters was highly effective in reducing the amount and accuracy of enemy fire against the transport helicopters; the gunships were here to stay.

The later UH-1B variants – which were delivered from October 1962 – took advantage of the increased power available in the improved T53-L-5 engine to carry the XM-6 Emerson 'quad gun' system. The flex guns, as they became known, were controlled by the co-pilot via a flexible pantographic sight mounted on the cabin roof and could be depressed 85 degrees and elevated 10 degrees. They could also be moved sideways 10 degrees inboard and 70 degrees outward and were fed by a dozen 500-round ammunition boxes mounted on the rear cabin floor. With the two door gunners each armed with a standard M-60 machine gun and the jury-rigged rocket system designed for the UH-1A model, the UH-1B had become a formidable fire support platform.

> "The Huey had become a formidable fire support platform"

Following a request from US advisers for a medical evacuation capability, the 57th Medical Detachment (Helicopter Ambulance) was deployed to Nha Trang and Qui Nhon with the first of thousands of medevac Hueys arriving on May 2, 1962.

The plan was for the medevac helicopters to operate alongside Detachment 3 of the Pacific Air Rescue Centre, which was established at Tan Son Nhut on April 1. The unit consisted of only three officers and two non-commissioned officers and was without any search and rescue aircraft. These were not forthcoming because of the official government position: the Air Force was not supposed to be undertaking combat operations, therefore a search and rescue force could not be justified!

The de Havilland Canada C-7 Caribou was designed to operate from the short, rough airstrips that the Provider was unable to use. Whereas the Provider was limited to 11% of the airfields, the Caribou could fly into 77% of all airstrips in South Vietnam

This C-123K Provider is from the 19th Air Commando Squadron, 315th Air Commando Wing at Phan Rang. The Air Commando units were later renamed as Special Operations units

## Boosting numbers

On May 23, the 73rd Aviation Company arrived in Saigon with its two-seater Cessna O-1F Bird Dogs. Soon the 32 aircraft were spread in 15 different locations around South Vietnam; their main role being reconnaissance but they were also used for artillery adjustment, target acquisition, command and control, message pickup, medical evacuation and radio relay. Over the following 14 months they would record over 41,000 hours of flying time.

A second C-123 Provider transport squadron, the 777th Tactical Control Squadron, arrived at Da Nang Air Base in June under the codename *Saw Buck II.* Their 16 aircraft joined those of the 346th TCS (codename *Mule Train*) flying daily missions as a part of the Southeast Asia Airlift System.

The deployment of the Army's 1st Aviation Company to Southeast Asia on July 23, 1962 went a long way to improve the tactical airlift system. Initially their de Havilland Canada C-7 Caribou aircraft were based in Thailand, but in December they redeployed to Vung Tau in South Vietnam, were they were joined in July 1963 by the C-7s of the 61st Aviation Company.

The Caribou was designed to operate from the short, rough airstrips that the Provider was unable to use and was an ideal aircraft for counter-insurgency work. It could clear a 50ft barrier after a take-off run of 360m or land over the same obstacle with a distance of 375m. Even the old Southeast Asia hands were impressed when the Caribou made its unbelievably slow, steep approach to some of the primitive airstrips. Whereas the Provider was limited to 11% of the airfields, the Caribou could fly into 77% of all airstrips in South Vietnam.

## Mohawk

After a storm of controversy in the Pentagon, the US Army deployed the six Grumman OV-1 Mohawk aircraft of the 23rd Special Warfare Aviation Detachment to Vietnam in September 1962; for the purpose of providing air surveillance in support of ARVN forces. The Mohawks were initially based at Nha Trang, supporting the ARVN 9th Division and the Railway Security Agency.

Visual and Photographic reconnaissance by this twin-turbine aircraft produced a wealth of intelligence for the units they supported and hundreds of structures, most of them camouflaged, were detected

The Forward Air Controllers in their Cessna O-1 Bird Dogs and the Air Liaison Officers on the ground were the last elements in the air-ground operations system. The FAC would ensure that the ground-attack aircraft delivered their ordnance in the right place, usually marking the target area themselves with rockets mounted under their wings *(USAF Museum)*

Two of the aircraft introduced to the theatre in 1962 are seen together – with a C-7 Caribou refuelling a thirsty OV-1 Mohawk *(USAF Museum)*

After a storm of controversy in the Pentagon, the Army deployed six Grumman OV-1 Mohawk aircraft of the 23rd Special Warfare Aviation Detachment to Vietnam in September 1962, for the purpose of providing air surveillance in support of ARVN forces. They were equipped with side-looking airborne radar

in Viet Cong base areas. At the same time, hundreds of people were sighted in suspect areas, and because of the detailed familiarity of Mohawk crews with the local situation and activity patterns, some of the people sighted could be positively identified as insurgents. One of the unique advantages of the Mohawk in reconnaissance was its noise-to-speed ratio, which allowed the aircraft to get within observation distance of people on the ground without alerting them to its presence.

When the Mohawks deployed to Vietnam, their rules of engagement specified that a Vietnamese observer would be on board during all operational flights; that the aircraft would be armed with only 0.5in machine guns and that this armament would be used only when required to defend against a hostile attack. Although there was no standard armament for the OV-1s, various weapons were eventually carried, including rockets and napalm.

Between October 16, 1962 and March 15, 1963, the 23rd Special Warfare Aviation Detachment flew more than 2,000 hours and 785 combat support missions. Mohawks delivered defensive fire 27 times, and two aircraft were lost.

## Year end

By the end of 1962 almost 4,000 Viet Cong had been killed or wounded and VNAF aircraft had damaged or destroyed more than 11,500 structures belonging to the insurgents. They had also sunk over 1,500 boats – a significant accomplishment in the Mekong Delta region of Vietnam where boats represent virtually the only means of transport.

Against these figures the VNAF and US Army had begun to suffer their first losses, as had the *Farm Gate* and other USAF aircraft.

Viet Cong anti-aircraft fire, particularly below 1,000ft, became more effective as they received more Soviet or Chinese-made 12.7mm heavy machine guns and by the end of 1962 the USAF had lost half a dozen aircraft to enemy ground fire.

As the year drew to a close, President Kennedy authorised an increase in strength of the *Farm Gate* detachment and five more T-28s, ten B-26s and two C-47s were despatched on New Year's Eve. At that time there were 11,300 US military advisers in South Vietnam while the strength of the South Vietnamese armed forces stood at 243,000 men.

# THE RISE OF EAGLE FLIGHTS

**Following a disastrous start, the ARVN and US advisers soon streamlined the helicopter borne air assault process in 1963. However, the year was marred by political coups and the loss of a leader**

**The disastrous attempt to seize a Viet Cong radio transmitter on January 2 was hampered when a VNAF Skyraider air strike accidentally hit a friendly unit, causing numerous casualties** *(USAF Museum)*

The new year began with a major defeat for the Army of the Republic of the Vietnam (ARVN) when the 7th division pressed on with an operation, on January 2, to seize a Viet Cong radio transmitter in the Plain of Reeds even though there was no tactical air support available.

The division commander believed that the transmitter was guarded by only one company of Viet Cong but the village was actually defended by 400 men of the 514th Viet Cong (Regular) Battalion, equipped with automatic rifles and several heavy machine guns. As the heli-borne force flared over the landing zone, the Viet Cong opened fire and within minutes five helicopters were destroyed and nine damaged.

The Air Operations Centre diverted two Douglas A-1 Skyraiders to the scene, but artillery firing through the airspace forced the aircraft to delay their attack.

To add to the confusion, Vietnamese Forward Air Controllers were unable to direct air strikes with any accuracy and the American advisers had extreme difficulty persuading the ARVN troops to advance, allowing the enemy to withdraw under the cover of darkness – but not before a VNAF air strike had accidentally hit a friendly unit, causing numerous casualties.

As the Viet Cong began to withdraw, the ARVN IV Corps Commander ordered three companies of Vietnamese paratroopers to be dropped by C-123s. He directed them to the west of Ap Bac, although the enemy were withdrawing to the east and the confused ARVN troops spent the night engaging each other in fire fights while the enemy escaped.

By the morning, friendly casualties stood at 65 ARVN troops and three American advisers killed and 100 ARVN and six American advisers wounded. According to the Viet Cong, the victory boosted their flagging morale and was a major turning point in their war effort.

## *Patricia Lynn*

On March 9, one of the US Army Mohawks crashed near the top of a 6,000ft mountain in the Central Highlands. Two Marine H-34 helicopters attempted to land a rescue team at the crash site, but as one hovered close to the treetops it crashed, killing two of the occupants. The next morning another H-34 suffered the same fate, injuring two of the crew. These sorts of fiascos illustrated the need for a properly trained and equipped Search and Rescue organisation, but such a thing was almost two years in the future.

A month later, on April 15, two Martin RB-57E Canberras were deployed to Tan Son Nhut Air Base as part of Project *Patricia Lynn*. They were equipped with both infrared and panoramic cameras and the photographs that they brought back enabled image analysts to identify Viet Cong base camps, small arms factories and storage and training areas that were not otherwise detected by the naked eye.

The Canberras joined the Tan Son Nhut RF-101 force and were later supplemented by two *Farm Gate* RB-26s, modified for night photography, although they were withdrawn early in 1964 due to structural fatigue.

A host of CH-21 Shawnees come in to land while a flight of UH-1B gunships follow on behind them

Fairchild C-123s were used for para-dropping both troops and supplies *(USAF Museum)*

Martin RB-57E from Project Patricia Lynn in the revetments at Dan Nang AB, South Vietnam. The aircraft was built as a B-57E (S/N 55-4264) before being converted to RB-57 standard. This aircraft was lost on October 25, 1968 *(USAF Museum)*

A Martin RB-57E taxies at Tan Son Nhut AB, Vietnam with a C-123 on final approach for landing in the background. Recce Canberras were equipped with both infrared and panoramic cameras and the photographs that they brought back enabled image analysts to identify Viet Cong base camps, small arms factories and storage and training areas that were not otherwise detected by the naked eye

## Psychological warfare

Two days after the B-57s arrived, President Ngo Dinh Diem (of the Republic of Vietnam) instituted his Chieu Hoi Open Arms campaign, a psychological (PSYOPS) warfare programme designed to persuade members of the Viet Cong to defect.

This was carried out through leaflet drops or by using aircraft and helicopters equipped with loudspeakers to broadcast appeals for the guerrillas to surrender and return to their families. These, often emotional, appeals together with a guarantee of clemency and financial inducements, persuaded many Viet Cong to defect to the government and some even worked as scouts for ARVN and later, American combat units.

The Chieu Hoi campaign continued right through the war until, to the eternal shame of the CIA, the records of all the defectors were abandoned for the North Vietnamese to find as Saigon fell in 1975.

The alternating *Water Glass* deployments of all-weather interceptors to Tan Son Nhut were terminated in May, due to the low probability of an enemy air attack and base overcrowding. A series of no-notice test deployments of Pacific Air Force (PACAF) F-102s took place later in the year, under the new codename *Candy Machine.*

> "Confused Vietnamese troops spent the night engaging each other in fire fights"

## New 'Hueys'

The five original US Army CH-21 Transportation Companies began to reequip with the UH-1B version of Bell's Iroquois in the summer of 1963. The first unit to receive the new 'Hueys' was the 81st Transportation Company at Pleiku, which was renamed the 119th Aviation Company (Air Mobile Light) on June 14. By the end of the year most of the companies had re-equipped as the CH-21s were phased out of the Army inventory.

With the arrival of the UH-1Bs, the structure of the Transportation Companies was changed and they were re-designated Aviation Companies. Each Company was made up of three platoons: two troop-lift or 'slick' platoons, (so named because their UH-1Bs lacked the drag-producing armament kits) and a platoon of UH-1B gunships. A total of 25 UH-1Bs were assigned to each Company; eight for each platoon plus a reserve.

When the UH-1B was first introduced in Vietnam, it usually carried ten or sometimes eleven combat-equipped Vietnamese soldiers. An investigation determined that the average helicopter was grossly over-loaded with this many soldiers. With ten soldiers averaging 167lbs and their full load, a US Army crew of four, armour plating, a tool box, a container of water, a case of emergency rations, weapons and armoured vests for the crew, the Huey grossed 8,700lbs – some 2,100lbs over the maximum operational weight. Not only that, the

The Chieu Hoi Open Arms campaign was a psychological warfare programme designed to persuade members of the Viet Cong to defect. This was carried out by leaflet drops (as seen here being conducted by a Cessna O-2) or by using aircraft and helicopters equipped with loudspeakers *(USAF Museum)*

The alternating *Water Glass* deployments of all-weather interceptors to Tan Son Nhut were terminated in May, due to the low probability of an enemy air attack and base overcrowding. A series of no-notice test deployments of Pacific Air Force (PACAF) F-102s took place later in the year, under the new codename *Candy Machine*. *(USAF Museum)*

centre of gravity had shifted beyond safe limits. As a consequence, the standard procedure was to limit the UH-1B to eight combat troops, except in the gravest emergencies.

Apart from the early XM-6 system [see 1962 chapter] there were three basic weapon kits for the armed helicopter platoons during the early and middle years of US involvement in Vietnam. The XM-16 system combined the XM-6 quad guns with Navy and Air Force XM-157 seven-shot rocket pods. These became standard equipment in all gunship platoons, but the tubes were not individually replaceable meaning repairs took longer to complete.

The Army later developed the XM-158 launcher with separate, removable tubes and safer rear loading. The impressive XM-3 system consisted of 48 rockets mounted in four six-tube banks either side of the helicopter. They were fired by either pilot or co-pilot through a Mk VIII sight and could be launched in pairs, ripples of six pairs, or in a massive burst of all 24 pairs, delivering 480lbs of explosives.

An XM-5 grenade launcher could also be mounted in a ball turret under the nose of the Huey and could fire 40mm grenades similar to those used in the infantry M-79 grenade launcher. The original system could fire a total of 150 rounds; 75 in a box in the rear cabin and a further 75 in the chute system feeding the gun.

## Armed and heavy

The armament system brought the UH-1B up to its maximum gross weight, thereby eliminating it from a troop or cargo-carrying role. The UH-1B was not actually designed for an armed configuration and the weight of the armament reduced the manoeuvrability of the helicopter and induced sufficient drag to lower the maximum speed to around 80kts. As a result, the gunships could not overtake the airmobile force if they left the formation to attack targets en-route.

Apart from armament, the Utility Tactical Transport Helicopter Company (UTTHCO) tried and tested a wide range of tactics and formations. The basic fire team consisted of two gunships working together in support of each other and the troop transports. Several fire teams could be used together to support large formations, with some flying escort and the others going ahead to make pre-landing strikes at the landing zone (LZ) or to observe it prior to the main assault.

Some basic operating procedures became standard. When a target was identified, the escort leader determined whether it could be attacked under the rules of engagement and, if so, it was engaged at the maximum range of the gunships' weapons. This usually consisted of a continuous burst of machine gun fire throughout each firing run, reinforced when necessary by rocket fire. The flight pattern was planned so that by the time the lead gunship had completed its firing run, the next one was in position to engage the target. This tactic placed continuous fire on the target until it was neutralised.

This UH-1C 'Heavy Hog' is fitted with the XM-3 rocket system as well as the XM-5 grenade launcher mounted in a ball-turret under the nose of the Huey and could fire 40mm grenades similar to those used in the infantry M-79 grenade launcher. The original system could fire a total of 150 rounds; 75 in a box in the rear cabin and a further 75 in the chute feeding system feeding the gun

## Typical mission

Planning for an airmobile assault had evolved rapidly from the haphazard co-ordination witnessed in early 1962. Usually the Aviation Battalion would receive a mission request from the Corps Tactical Operations Centre and then assign it to one of the Aviation Companies. If time permitted, aerial reconnaissance was conducted by the airmobile company commanding officer, a representative of the Aviation Battalion and a representative from the supported unit.

Approach and departure routes were selected, condition and size of the LZ were noted while flight formations, checkpoints and altitudes to be flown were determined. The type of helicopter formation to be used en-route depended on the size and shape of the LZ and the company commander's requirements for disembarking his troops after landing. When an uninterrupted flow of troops into a small landing area was required, a modified trail formation could be used. The formation most frequently used was the 'V'. This proved to be versatile, easy to control and permitted landing of the flight in a minimum of time. The 'slicks' normally flew about 45 degrees to the side and rear of the lead ship and high enough to be out of the rotor wash.

During the critical approach phase, it was desirable to land all the helicopters simultaneously, although this could be difficult due to the stepped altitude of the formation, rotor wash encountered during descent and the difficulty in finding a suitable touchdown spot for each helicopter.

The terrain in the LZ sometimes slowed the disembarking of troops. In the Delta, water was sometimes chest deep and in the jungle areas the grass could be ten to 12ft high. For a 12-ship formation, two minutes was considered an average unloading time from the moment the first helicopter touched down until the last ship took off. In a 'hot' landing zone where the assault was opposed by the enemy, two minutes could seem like an eternity.

For obvious reasons the helicopters

Apart from armament, the Utility Tactical Transport Helicopter Company tried and tested a wide range of tactics and formations

**"This tactic placed continuous fire on the target until it was neutralised"**

▲ When the UH-1B was first introduced in Vietnam, it usually carried ten or sometimes eleven combat-equipped soldiers. An investigation determined that the average helicopter was grossly over-loaded with this many soldiers

◄ Huey gunships generally attacked targets by flying in pairs in a racetrack pattern, so that one gunship always had guns on target

would take off in a different direction from their approach and to lessen the possibility of fire being concentrated on a single ship, all helicopters attempted to depart at the same time.

## Eagle Flight

In an attempt to reduce the planning time required for executing an air assault mission, some of the earlier helicopter units developed an operation called an Eagle Flight. A typical Eagle Flight would consist of one armed Huey as the command and control ship, with the US Army aviation commander and the ARVN troop commander aboard; seven unarmed 'slicks' to transport the combat troops; five armed Huey gunships to give fire support and escort the slicks and one Huey usually designated as a medical evacuation ship. The Eagle Flights were usually on standby or sometimes airborne, searching for their own targets. Not only were the flights immediately available for missions with a minimum of planning, but they also provided the basis for larger operations.

By November 1963, all helicopter companies in South Vietnam had organised their own Eagle Flights and each company maintained at least one flight on an alert status. Vietnamese troop commanders were very enthusiastic about these operations, as they provided a close working relationship between the air and ground elements and, above all, were able to capitalise on the element of surprise which was so often lost in detailed planning with ARVN troops.

## Invader down

Although the new helicopter technology was proving phenomenally successful, the use of older generation aircraft was starting to be problematical.

During the summer the original *Farm Gate* detachment had been succeeded by the 1st Air Commando Squadron, which soon encountered problems with its World

War Two-era Douglas B-26 Invaders. Structural fatigue in the wings led to the fatal crash of a B-26 in August and the squadron was soon under instructions to avoid undue wing stress.

Elsewhere, although President Diem's armed forces were now performing better as a result of improved organisation and training by their US advisers, Diem was facing problems in Saigon. Buddhist demonstrations continued through the year and Diem decided it was time to teach them a lesson. On August 21, 1963 he sent his Special Forces and combat police to storm Buddhist pagodas throughout the country. Around 1,400 men, mostly monks, were dragged off to jail where they were beaten, half-starved and tortured.

The American Embassy was shocked and horrified and within a week the Kennedy Administration, on CIA advice, had let it be known that they would back the generals who had long been planning a coup against Diem. These were led by General Doung Van Minh ('Big Minh' as he became known to the Americans) and included General Tran Van Don, acting chief of the Joint General Staff and General Nguyen Khanh, commander of II Corps, north of Saigon.

## Coup d'état

On November 1, 1963, the generals launched their coup, spearheaded by two marine and two airborne battalions and backed by 30 tanks. They soon captured the radio station and other key buildings in Saigon, but Diem's loyal troops at the Presidential Palace put up a stiff resistance.

In the meantime, Wing Commander Nguyen Cao Ky (who had led the combined 'Dirty Thirty'/VNAF unit – see introduction) arrested the commander of the VNAF at Tan Son Nhut Air Base and sent two T-28s to attack the troops defending the palace. After they had fired only two rockets the garrison surrendered, but not before Diem and his brother Nhu had escaped through a secret tunnel. They were eventually discovered in a Catholic church in Cholon, the Chinese city-within-a-city on the edge of Saigon.

The brothers agreed to surrender following a guarantee of safe conduct and an armoured car was sent to collect them. Their arms were bound and they were thrown into the armoured car and then shot by a police officer. General Minh settled into the Presidential Palace as head of the Military Revolutionary Council and Ky was named as the new commander of the air force.

The new rulers began the wholesale dismissal of government officials loyal to Diem and this action, together with their lack of administrative experience, soon produced governmental paralysis. The Viet Cong took advantage of the disarray and launched numerous attacks throughout South Vietnam. The demoralised ARVN troops were no match for the enemy and suffered a number of defeats as a result.

> "In a 'hot' landing zone two minutes could seem like an eternity"

▲ **By the end of 1963, 58 Army helicopters had been lost to all causes in South Vietnam. Recovering downed helicopters would prove to be a difficult task, especially in enemy-controlled territory**

◄ **After the November 1 coup which saw the assassination of President Diem, General Minh moved into the Presidential Palace as head of the Military Revolutionary Council and Wing Commander Ky was named as the new commander of the air force**

In response to the coup, Cambodian Prince Norodom Sihanouk cancelled all American aid on November 20 and received four MiG jet fighters and 27 anti-aircraft guns from the Soviet Union. US activities within that country were to cease by January 15, 1964.

Shortly after the Vietnamese coup, the world was rocked by the death of another leader: on November 22 President John F Kennedy was shot and killed in Dallas, Texas. Vice-President Lyndon B Johnson was inaugurated as President shortly afterwards. The war in Vietnam would continue unabated.

By the end of the year, American strength in South Vietnam had reached 16,000 personnel with 117 USAF aircraft and 325 Army helicopters now based in the country. Casualties had also begun to mount with 18 USAF aircraft and 58 Army helicopters had been lost in combat and to other non-hostile causes.

# PRESIDENT JOHNSON DECLARES WAR ON THE NORTH

**Flying low over the jungle, an A-1 Skyraider drops 500lb bombs on a Viet Cong position below as smoke rises from a previous pass at the target, on December 26, 1964** *(USAF Museum)*

**In a year that saw seven changes of government in Vietnam and a new US President finding his feet, America widened the war against North Vietnam**

As with the previous year, 1964 did not get off to the best of starts. On January 18, the Army of the Republic of Vietnam (ARVN) launched the largest helicopter operation ever undertaken in South Vietnam up to that time. Operating in War Zone D, the airlift saw 115 helicopters carry 1,100 troops in an operation against the Viet Cong. The operation went smoothly but unfortunately not a single enemy soldier could be found!

Unsuccessful operations such as these, combined with continuing political instability, led to another coup on January 30. Major General Nguyen Khanh, a tough paratrooper and commander of I Corps, ousted General Minh ('Big Minh' – see previous chapter) and stated his intention to increase operations against the enemy. However, such was the state of Vietnamese politics and the desire of the generals to dabble in politics that by the end of 1964 there had been seven changes of government.

While the Vietnamese generals indulged in political manoeuvres, President Johnson settled himself in the executive chair at the White House and turned his attention to the war. On February 21, in one of his first public comments on the war, President Johnson warned Hanoi to end its support of insurgent forces in South Vietnam and Laos.

At this time he still supported the previous policy that the South Vietnamese and Laotian people were primarily responsible for their own defence. To this end, the first withdrawal of 1,000 US servicemen went on as planned. Among them were members of the famed 'Dirty Thirty' group of C-47 pilots and the US Army's 1st Aviation Company.

## Fatigued

Meanwhile, the 1st Air Commando Squadron (1st ACS) with its ageing ground-attack aircraft was in trouble. In February, two of its T-28s were shot down by ground fire and ten days later their B-26 Invader fleet was grounded due to structural fatigue.

General Jacob E Smart, the Commander-in-Chief of the Pacific Air Forces (PACAF), recommended deployment to South Vietnam of a B-57 light jet bomber squadron, but Secretary of Defence McNamara disagreed. He did agree, however, to equip a new VNAF squadron with Douglas A-1H Skyraiders and to replace the 1st ACS's T-28s and B-26s with 25 two-seater Skyraiders.

These decisions came too late for two USAF T-28 pilots and their Vietnamese crewmen. On March 24, one T-28 crashed after its wing sheared off during a bomb run and on April 9, a second T-28 ploughed into a rice paddy after both its wings fell off during a dive. The morale of the 1st ACS pilots understandably sagged, despite the loan of nine surplus T-28Bs from the VNAF.

On March 5, Secretary McNamara approved the deployment of Detachment 6 of the 1st Air Commando Wing to the Royal Thai Air Force Base (RTAFB) at Udorn. The detachment, known by the codename *Waterpump* consisted of four T-28s and 41 men and its mission was to train Laotian and Thai pilots and maintenance personnel. Not coincidentally, this unit also provided a source of US controlled aircraft to augment the small Royal Laotian Air Force and came directly under the control of US Ambassador Leonard Unger in Vientiane.

## *Yankee Team*

On March 16, all semblance of peace in Laos vanished as the Pathet Lao, with North Vietnamese backing, attacked across the Plain of Jars. As the Neutralist and Royal Laotian Government forces began to fall back, Washington approved the resumption of RF-101 Voodoo reconnaissance flights on May 19, under the codename *Yankee Team*. They were joined by US Navy RF-8A Crusader and RA-3B Skywarrior reconnaissance aircraft from the Seventh Fleet in the Gulf of Tonkin.

Photographic interpreters scrutinising *Yankee Team* photographs discovered that the Plain of Jars was bristling with weapons including 16 anti-aircraft sites noted with both 37mm and 57mm guns. Each gun was capable of firing 150 rounds per minute, and effective up to 4,500 and 15,000ft respectively. Since most reconnaissance missions were flown below 1,500ft, these powerful weapons were yet another threat to the unarmed reconnaissance pilots, who already had to contend with 12.7mm and 14.5mm heavy machine guns, with an effective range of 1,800ft and 3,000ft respectively.

## Flak trap

The threat was realised on June 6 when Corktip 920, a US Navy Vought RF-8A Crusader piloted by Lt Charles Klusmann, was shot down south of the village of Ban Ban, deep inside communist-controlled territory and only 20 miles from the North Vietnamese border.

An Air America C-123 and U-10 Helio-Courier aircraft were in the area and located

A Royal Lao Air Force T-28 departs on a bombing mission

Armourers loading AIM-9 Sidewinder missiles onto a Vought F-8 Crusader on the USS *Hancock* in the South China Sea

As the Neutralist and Royal Laotian Government forces began to fall back, Washington approved the resumption of RF-101 Voodoo reconnaissance flights on May 19, under the codename Yankee Team. This RF-101C captured its own shadow during a low-level run over a damaged bridge in North Vietnam

the pilot within an hour but it was two hours before Air America helicopters arrived at the crash scene.

As they approached, the entire area erupted in gunfire. The enemy had employed a tactic he would use often during the next ten years: the flak trap. The pilot would be allowed to call for help while the enemy positioned anti-aircraft weapons around the area and waited for the rescuers to arrive. In this case both helicopters were hit and two men critically wounded. They had to abandon the attempt and head for the nearest Lima site (landing strip and base area).

The following day Old Nick 110, an F-8D, was shot down in the same area while escorting an RF-8A on a reconnaissance mission. The pilot survived the ejection from his aircraft and spent a lonely night in the jungle evading the enemy. In the morning he heard the drone of aircraft above the foggy mist and fired a flare. An Air America H-34 descended below the clouds and snatched him to safety.

At this early stage of the war there was still no official co-ordinated Search and Rescue (SAR) organisation to assist pilots who were shot down over South Vietnam or Laos. Of the two countries, Laos was worse to get shot down in and at the time of writing almost 600 American personnel are still listed as missing there. Fortunately, Lt Klusmann, the pilot of Corktip 920, is not among them. After three months in captivity, he managed to escape and reach safety on foot.

> "The pilot survived the ejection and spent a lonely night in the jungle evading the enemy"

The day after Old Nick 110 was shot down, a retaliatory strike by eight USAF North American F-100 Super Sabres was authorised against the anti-aircraft sites at Xieng Khouang. From then, on all RF-101 missions were given F-100 escorts when their targets were on the Plain of Jars.

## Kien Long offensive

Back in South Vietnam, the Viet Cong began to expand its military operations and, at the same time, started to infiltrate regular North Vietnamese Army (NVA) units into the country.

On April 12, they launched an attack on the district capital of Kien Long on the Ca Mau peninsula. Despite valiant air-to-ground support provided by VNAF A-1H Skyraiders, the Viet Cong overran the city, killing 300 ARVN troops and leaving over 200 civilians dead or wounded. This defeat was followed by widespread terrorist attacks throughout the country, including a daring raid on May 2, when a Viet Cong underwater demolition team sank the USS *Card*, which had been unloading helicopters at the Saigon waterfront.

US Secretary of Defence McNamara visited Saigon in May and reiterated the administration's policy that all US airmen should be out of combat within a matter of months. He also decided that USAF pilots could no longer fly combat missions, even with a Vietnamese observer on board, despite authorising the Air Force to equip a second Air Commando Squadron with A-1E Skyraiders.

To balance this loss of USAF strike support, McNamara directed that four VNAF squadrons should be equipped with A-1H model Skyraiders as soon as possible and that two more squadrons should be formed to replace the USAF units scheduled for withdrawal. Meanwhile, the situation at the 1st ACS began to improve as it received the first six A-1Es at the end of May to replace its T-28s and B-26s. The Skyraiders were well suited to the counter-insurgency role, with a 7,000lb bomb load, four 20mm cannon, heavy armour plating and an excellent loiter capability.

## Search & Rescue

June 1964 saw the first efforts to establish a dedicated Search and Rescue organisation when two Kaman HH-43B Huskie helicopters from the 33rd Air Rescue Squadron at Okinawa arrived at the RTAFB at Nakhon Phanom on the Thai-Laos border.

At the same time, two Grumman HU-16B Albatross amphibians were detached to Korat RTAFB to act as airborne rescue control ships and three HU-16Bs were sent

**The Skyraiders supplied to the Vietnamese Air Force were well suited to the counter-insurgency role, with a 7,000lb bomb load, four 20mm cannon, heavy armour plating and an excellent loiter capability**

**An American pilot receives a briefing prior to boarding the VNAF Skyraider behind him**

**When US Navy Vought RF-8A Crusader pilot Lt Charles Klusmann, was shot down he was located by an Air America U-10 Helio-Courier within an hour but it was two hours before Air America helicopters arrived at the crash scene** *(USAF Museum)*

to Da Nang in South Vietnam for rescue duties in the Gulf of Tonkin.

While the arrival of the first SAR helicopters raised the morale of the Yankee Team reconnaissance pilots, the effect was not entirely warranted. The HH-43B was a short-range crash-rescue helicopter and the only one in the USAF inventory. It had a relatively small radius of action of 140 miles at most and was thus unable to provide SAR cover for the Plain of Jars. (An aircraft damaged by anti-aircraft fire over the Plain of Jars had to be flown at least 50 miles south to be within range of any rescue helicopters based at Nakhon Phanom.)

As the communist offensive in Northern Laos continued, it became obvious that the SAR assets were woefully inadequate to cover US air operations and Air America was asked to provide search and rescue support when needed. Air America's H-34 fleet had dwindled from 16 to four and in July they asked the Department of Defence for more. These were transferred to them from the United States Marine Corps (USMC), despite Marine protestations.

The objections were understandable as the Medium Helicopter Squadron HMM-362 was the only USMC squadron in Vietnam and was the resident Operation *Shufly* squadron at Da Nang. It had recently been given the job of training Vietnamese pilots and crews on the Sikorsky UH-34 and the Department of Defence directive came at the same time as HMM-362 was ordered to turn its 24 H-34s over to the VNAF, pending delivery of replacements from Sikorsky.

## Bloody July

The Viet Cong turned July 1964 into the bloodiest month to date. On July 6, it attacked the Nam Dong Special Forces camp in I Corps, killing 55 ARVN troops, two US Rangers and an Australian adviser. Although a C-47 flare ship illuminated the area, no VNAF strike aircraft were available to respond to calls for help.

A fortnight later, the Viet Cong ambushed 400 ARVN troops in Chuong Thien Province in the Delta. It took an hour for a VNAF Forward Air Controller to arrive over the battle site and another 30 minutes before strike aircraft arrived from Bien Hoa. Only 82 ARVN soldiers walked away from the ambush.

In order to lessen the chances of another disaster, senior US Army advisers would from now on hold a daily pre-planning conference with their USAF counterparts to ensure maximum use of the strike aircraft. An emergency VNAF air request net was also established to allow ARVN commanders to direct calls for help straight to an air support centre, bypassing intermediate ARVN headquarters.

As the month came to an end, it was obvious that despite the assistance of over 16,000 American military advisers the South Vietnamese Army was unable to halt – let alone defeat – the Viet Cong insurgency. Regular North Vietnamese Army units were now infiltrating the South and it was time for the USA to raise the stakes.

In June 1964 two Grumman HU-16B Albatross amphibians were detached to Korat RTAFB to act as airborne rescue control ships and three HU-16Bs were sent to Da Nang in South Vietnam for rescue duties in the Gulf of Tonkin

Led by a Marine adviser a company of South Vietnamese troops board H-34 helicopters from HMM-163 at Tam Ky

## Johnson's War

On July 31, the US Navy began to conduct DeSoto intelligence gathering patrols off the coast of North Vietnam in the Gulf of Tonkin. This was in order to update their overall intelligence picture in case they had to operate against North Vietnam. The destroyer USS *Maddox* picked up the necessary equipment and personnel and headed north. At the same time, CIA-trained South Vietnamese commando squads operating from patrol boats attacked North Vietnamese installations on Hon Me and Hon Ngu islands, 60 miles from the coast at the 19th Parallel.

Although the *Maddox* was 100 miles to the southeast at this time, the raid stirred up a hornets' nest of electronic radio and radar activity, sufficient to bring a smile to the face of the hardest intelligence gathering equipment operator.

Thirty-six hours later, on the morning of August 2, the *Maddox* received intelligence indicating possible action from North Vietnam. At 15.00hrs, while the *Maddox* was still in international waters, three North Vietnamese patrol boats came out to attack. As they engaged with torpedoes and machine-gun fire, the *Maddox* requested assistance from the aircraft carrier USS *Ticonderoga*. Four F-8E Crusaders from Navy Fighter Squadron VF-53 were launched and together with gunfire from the destroyer, managed to sink or badly damage all three patrol boats.

High-level discussions in Washington led to a decision to send the M*addox* back into the area two days later, together with the destroyer USS *Turner Joy*. They were instructed to assert their right to sail in international waters up to eight miles from the North Vietnamese coast.

By 20.00hrs that night the destroyers were being buffeted by thunderstorms as they sailed through the darkness. The sonar on *Maddox* was functioning erratically and atmospheric conditions were distorting the signals reaching the radar on both ships. The *Maddox* intercepted a North Vietnamese message, which was interpreted as implying that an attack was imminent and eight Crusaders from the *Ticonderoga* were summoned.

The aircraft failed to spot any attackers but following a number of suspected contacts on the surface search radar, both ships opened fire on what they thought were torpedo boats only 6,000 yards from the *Maddox*.

Torpedo noises were heard on the *Maddox's* sonar and the crew of the *Turner Joy* reported seeing the wake of a torpedo passing about 300ft to port. Captain J J Herrick, the task force commander, reported to his superiors that they were under attack and the message was passed on up the line to the President himself. By midnight, radar contact with the enemy had ceased.

Neither destroyer was damaged, although the USS *Turner Joy* claimed three enemy boats sunk. As they left the area, their commanders began to have doubts and suggested a thorough daylight reconnaissance by aircraft before any further action.

**In response to the Gulf of Tonkin incident, aircraft carrier USS *Constellation* was ordered to proceed to the North Vietnamese coast at full speed. Among the first aircraft to launch on the retaliatory attack on August 5 were Douglas A-4 Skyhawks**

**When the USS *Maddox* was 'attacked' in the Gulf of Tonkin in 1964 it was a turning point in the war** *(US DoD)*

**Two days after the reprisal raid for the Gulf of Tonkin incident 30 MiG-15s and MiG-17s from China flew into Phuc Yen airfield near Hanoi. These two are parked in revetments at the edge of the airfield**

The President and his advisers were convinced, however, that an attack had taken place and authorised retaliation against the North. After the war it became clear that no attack had taken place that night, but the allegation had given President Johnson the excuse to widen American action against North Vietnam.

## "Launch Pierce Arrow"

In response to the Gulf of Tonkin incident, aircraft carrier USS *Constellation* had been ordered to leave Hong Kong on August 2 and to proceed to the North Vietnamese coast at full speed. Aboard both the USS *Ticonderoga* and USS *Constellation*, crewmen hurried to arm and prepare their F-8 Crusaders, Douglas A-4 Skyhawks and Douglas A-1 Skyraiders for a 10.30hrs launch on August 5.

As President Johnson sat down before the television cameras to announce the raid to the nation, a message was flashed across the Pacific: 'Launch Pierce Arrow'.

Shortly afterwards, 64 naval aircraft struck four North Vietnamese patrol boat bases, destroying or damaging 25 boats: half the North Vietnamese fleet. The fuel-oil storage tanks at Vinh, just north of the DMZ were struck, destroying 10% of the North's oil supply in one go.

The raid was not without cost however, as two Navy aircraft were lost. Before President Johnson had finished his speech, Lt Everett Alvarez, a 26-year-old Skyhawk pilot from the USS *Constellation*, was afloat in the water off Hon Gai with a fractured back. He became the first of 600 airmen to be captured during the war and was to spend eight years as a prisoner.

Two days after the reprisal raid, on August 7, Congress passed the Southeast Asia Resolution, commonly called the Tonkin Gulf Resolution. This crucial and controversial document declared that:

"The United States regards as vital to its national interest and to world peace the maintenance of international peace and security in Southeast Asia. Consonant with Constitution of the United States and the Charter of the United Nations and in accordance with its obligations under the Southeast Asia Collective Defense Treaty, the United States is, therefore, prepared, as the President determines, to take all necessary steps, including the use of armed force, to assist any member or protocol state of the Southeast Asia Collective Defense Treaty requesting assistance in defense of its freedom.

"This resolution shall expire when the President shall determine that the peace and security of the area is reasonably assured by international conditions created by action of the United Nations or otherwise, except that it may be terminated earlier by concurrent resolution of the Congress."

As such, Congress gave President Johnson and his advisers the power to direct an undeclared war against the North Vietnam.

## 'Fast/Full Squeeze'

By this time the Joint Chiefs of Staff (JCS) had already drawn up contingency plans for American air operations against North Vietnam and they recommended a 'fast/full squeeze' hard-hitting, 16-day air campaign against 94 targets in North Vietnam, to establish US air superiority and destroy Hanoi's ability to continue to support operations against South Vietnam.

The military's view was to hit hard

A B-57 using a starter cartridge to fire up its engine while ground crew stand by with a fire extinguisher. Note the lack of protective revetments on the Bien Hoa ramp

Following the Tonkin Gulf Incident dozens of F-100 Super Sabres were sent to South Vietnam

and right away. However, the Johnson Administration favoured a campaign of gradually increasing military pressures that would hopefully act as both 'carrot and stick' to induce North Vietnam to settle the war on US terms.

No doubt Johnson was reluctant to commit himself to an all-out campaign, with US elections only two months away, and he was also concerned that the destruction of Hanoi's war-making capability might bring China and Russia into the conflict. The JCS were aware of the possibility and assumed that Communist Chinese ground troops might be used to aid the North Vietnamese, as had occurred in Korea, and that Russia would provide increased military support, including technicians and modern weaponry. They were confident, however, that the USA and its allies could deal adequately with such eventualities. The view of the President and his advisers prevailed and it was they, not the military who sat down to direct the air war, on a case-by-case and day by day basis.

The North Vietnamese were not impressed by the decisions of Congress, nor the reprisal raid on 5 August. Two days later they deployed 30 MiG-15s and MiG-17s from China into Phuc Yen airfield and ordered the 325th Division of the North Vietnamese Army down the Ho Chi Minh Trail.

## Canberra catastrophe

The first USAF aircraft to deploy to South Vietnam following the Tonkin Gulf incident were Martin B-57B Canberra bombers from the 8th and 13th Bomb Squadrons. The 20 aircraft had been put on standby at Clark AFB in the Philippines and during the evening of August 4, they were ordered to deploy to Bien Hoa AB as soon as possible. The squadrons took the order literally and within hours the five flights of four aircraft had taken off and were en route to Vietnam.

The aircraft arrived over the unfamiliar Bien Hoa field in darkness and with a 700ft ceiling of monsoon weather. Uncertainties after landing caused one aircraft to delay on the runway, whereupon it was struck from behind by a second aircraft with brake failure and damaged beyond repair.

Another B-57 blew both main tyres on landing and the blocked runway caused the remaining jets to divert to Tan Son Nhut a few miles away. One B-57 did not arrive; it crashed a few miles short of the runway while on a straight-in TACAN approach. The crash site was in Viet Cong-controlled territory but the reason for the crash was never satisfactorily determined.

The B-57 was a welcome addition to the USAF inventory in South Vietnam. It was armed with either eight machine guns or four 20mm cannon and could carry an impressive bomb load both on its underwing pylons and in its internal bomb bay. They could also carry eight 5in or 28 2.75in rockets, and this could be doubled if the underwing pylons were used.

Unfortunately, the Canberras were not used in combat for some time following their deployment. The USA was still abiding by the Geneva Agreement of 1954, which stipulated that no new military weaponry would be introduced in Vietnam by either side. It would be six months before the restriction was lifted and the B-57s were flown into combat.

Other squadrons were also on the move: Strike Force One Buck involved the deployment of 17 North American F-100 Super Sabres from the 614th Tactical

Republic F-105D-30-RE 62-4234 in flight over Vietnam with a full bomb load

One deployment went almost unnoticed during the month of August. The first HH-43F rescue helicopters arrived at Bien Hoa and Da Nang to relieve the HH-43Bs

Fighter Squadron (TFS) to Clark AFB on August 4 and 18 more arrived the next day from the 522nd TFS.

Two months later, the 614th TFS, a part of the 401st Tactical Fighter Wing (TFW) flew its F-100s on to Da Nang; six more RF-101C Voodoos were sent to Tan Son Nhut AB to increase the *Able Mabel* detachment to 12 and Republic F-105 Thunderchiefs from the 18th TFW based on Okinawa moved into Thailand.

## Enter the Thud

Within a week of the Tonkin Gulf incident, eight F-105Ds had been standing on alert at Korat RTAFB on temporary duty (TDY) and their first combat mission took place before the end of August, when four Thuds (as the type had been nicknamed) from the 36th TFS were scrambled on a rescue combat air patrol (RESCAP).

An aircraft had been reported downed over the Plain of Jars in Laos, but when the F-105s arrived, they found an Air America C-7 Caribou orbiting the area, whose crew knew nothing about a bailout, but were receiving anti-aircraft fire and asked the F-105s to knock out the enemy gun site.

Nobody was sure of the enemy position and the F-105s decided to make strafing runs in the general area to tempt the enemy to show his hand. On the second pass they did just that…

Lt Dave Graben pressed the firing button as his big fighter hurtled toward the ground, spewing bursts of 20mm cannon fire from its Vulcan cannon at a rate of 6,000 rounds per minute. Suddenly, in the pilot's words, "red golf balls" streaked upward from the communists 37mm anti-aircraft guns and the Thunderchief shuddered as the shells hit home.

Graben pulled out of the steep dive and jettisoned all of his external stores and lit the afterburner to initiate a steep climb. The aircraft was vibrating badly and a red fire warning light came on as the pilot levelled out at 16,000ft. Luck was with him that day though, as the warning light went out and the Thunderchief stayed in one piece to make a perfect landing back at Korat.

The tail of the aircraft had been hit by two shells and there were also several shrapnel holes in the rear of the aircraft, but it had brought its pilot safely home. The Thud would continue to bring pilots home, often with more severe damage than that suffered by Dave Graben, and the type was soon in the forefront of the air war against North Vietnam.

August would also see the first new HH-43F rescue helicopters arrive at both Bien Hoa and Da Nang to relieve the ageing HH-43Bs. The newer model had a more powerful engine, titanium armour plating and a 350US Gal self-sealing fuel tank to extend its range.

The HH-43Fs were still inadequate for the combat rescue mission, but six more months would pass before the first Sikorsky CH-3C helicopters, on loan from the Tactical Air Command, would arrive in Thailand.

The US Army also saw a boost in aircraft numbers with the last CH-21 Shawnees retired mid-summer, to be replaced by 250 UH-1 Iroquois. The only other Army helicopter in use was the CH-37 Mojave cargo helicopter – of which nine were employed – but the Army had access to 147 fixed wing aircraft including 53 Bird Dogs, 20 U-6A Beavers, nine U-8 Seminoles, six OV-1 Mohawks, 32 C-7 Caribou and 27 U-1 Otters. Within a year though, the Army aviation inventory would expand beyond all expectations as the Airmobile Division concept was put into practice.

## Base attack

Overnight on October 31/November 1, the Viet Cong infiltrated to within 250 yards of the perimeter wire at Bien Hoa AB and silently set up six 81mm mortars. Shortly after midnight they fired around 70 rounds into the base and departed, undetected.

Twenty B-57s were parked wingtip to wingtip on the ramp and five were totally destroyed, along with an HH-43F and four

A CH-37 Mojave hovers over a downed CH-21 while the crewmen attach the hoisting sling

VNAF Skyraiders. All of the other 15 B-57s were damaged. Four Americans were killed and 72 others wounded.

The JCS and the US Ambassador in South Vietnam strongly recommended retaliatory action against North Vietnam, but the White House declined; it was the eve of the 1964 Presidential elections.

The JCS proposed an initial 24 to 36-hour period of air strikes in Laos and low-level air reconnaissance south of the 19th Parallel in North Vietnam, to provide cover while US security forces were introduced to protect US bases and installations in South Vietnam. This would be followed by three days of B-52 strikes against Phuc Yen and other airfields as well as major fuel facilities in the Hanoi/Haiphong area. Subsequent strikes would be on infiltration routes and transportation-related targets in the North, together with raids against other military and industrial targets.

At this time, air defences in North Vietnam were minimal. Apart from the few recently arrived MiGs, the aircraft inventory comprised just 30 trainer and 50 transport aircraft and four light helicopters.

Only Gia Lam airfield at Hanoi and Cat Bi airfield at Haiphong were capable of sustained jet operations, although Phuc Yen was nearly completed. Kien Long near Haiphong and Dong Hoi, just north of the DMZ, also had hard-surfaced runways capable of supporting jet aircraft. There were only 700 conventional anti-aircraft weapons and no surface-to-air missiles. The North Vietnamese radar tracking capability was also limited and consisted of only 20 early warning sets with very little capability for definitive tracking.

The US airstrikes would have been virtually unopposed and, launched with the element of surprise, they would have achieved the maximum success with a minimum number of losses.

Such attacks might well have persuaded North Vietnam to cease its aggression in the South. However, eight more years would pass before the USA launched anything resembling an all-out attack on North Vietnam, and during that time the North Vietnamese would build the largest, most powerful air defence system in the world.

**Overnight on October 31/November 1, the Viet Cong mortared Bien Hoa air base. Twenty B-57s were parked wingtip to wingtip on the ramp and five were totally destroyed, along with an HH-43F and four VNAF Skyraiders. All of the other 15 B-57s were damaged. Four Americans were killed and 72 others wounded *(USAF Museum)***

## Limited action

It would be December before President Johnson approved a series of limited armed reconnaissance missions against enemy lines of communication in eastern Laos. The first mission of Operation *Barrel Roll* took place on December 17, when Navy aircraft from the carrier USS *Ranger* conducted an armed reconnaissance patrol over likely infiltration routes. The A-1H Skyraiders were escorted by McDonnell F-4B Phantoms and followed by RF-8A reconnaissance aircraft and were authorised to strike communist supply vehicles or other targets of opportunity. The purpose of these early *Barrel Roll* missions was mainly political and from the beginning, Secretary McNamara allowed only two flights of four aircraft per week.

On Christmas Eve the Viet Cong blew up the Brink Hotel bachelor officers' quarters in Saigon, killing two Americans and injuring 71 others. There were repeated requests for a retaliatory airstrike against North Vietnam but the Johnson administration refused.

Three days later, the Viet Cong's newly formed 9th Division (which had been supplied with Soviet and Chinese weapons) attacked Binh Gia village, south east of Saigon. The battle led to the virtual destruction of the ARVN's 33rd Ranger and 4th Marine Battalions. The Viet Cong later boasted that the battle marked the end of the insurgency phase of its campaign and the beginning of conventional field operations.

The end of the year was marked by very heavy fighting but VNAF and USAF Skyraiders performed well and the air support units claimed 2,500 Viet Cong killed in November and December. A further 1,700 were killed by government troops but the enemy losses were soon replenished from the 30,000 to 40,000 infiltrators who had flowed into the south through Laos over the preceding three years.

# SEARCHING FOR SAMs, BUSTING BRIDGES AND DOWNING MIGs

**The first Navy aircraft to be brought down by a surface-to-air missile (SAM) was an A-4E, which was lost on August 13, 1965** *(US Navy)*

**1965 was the year the rules of engagement were relaxed and the war in Vietnam escalated. It would also be the year pilots were introduced to the perils of surface-to-air missiles**

It would be early 1965 before US military commanders finally convinced President Johnson that stronger action was needed against North Vietnam – and an opportunity to apply extra force arose on February 7.

In the early hours of the morning, the Viet Cong attacked the American compound and airstrip at Camp Holloway near Pleiku, killing eight and wounding 100 others; five helicopters were also destroyed. An hour later the Viet Cong attacked and set fire to aviation fuel storage tanks at Tuy Hoa airfield.

President Johnson ordered all US military dependents to leave Vietnam as he 'cleared the decks' and ordered a retaliatory raid against North Vietnam.

At midday Operation *Flaming Dart* I began as 49 A-1 Skyraiders and F-8 Crusaders took off from the decks of the USS *Coral Sea* and *Ranger*. Their target was the North Vietnamese Army barracks and guerrilla training establishment at Dong Hoi.

In an attempt to boost South Vietnamese morale, the Vietnamese Air Force (VNAF) was invited to participate in the operation but when their force of 24 Skyraiders arrived over Dong Hoi they found the US Navy attack in full swing so decided to find another target to punish.

Led by Air Marshall Ky, the chief of the VNAF himself, the South Vietnamese contingent headed towards the Vinhlinh area, where they found a target in the form of the headquarters of an anti-aircraft regiment. Needless to say, the return fire was ferocious and every one of the VNAF aircraft received hits. Air Marshal Ky was grazed by a bullet and two pilots were forced to bail out over the sea.

The VNAF attack caused some friction between Saigon and Washington as the target had not been authorised, but Ky lost no sleep over this; he knew that there was a war going on.

## Air Force airpower

The following day the USAF joined the operation and 30 *Farm Gate* A-1 Skyraiders (accompanied by F-100 Super Sabres flying flak suppression missions) struck the barracks at Chap Le.

President Johnson, emphasising that the air strikes were reprisals for earlier attacks, reiterated that the USA sought no wider war. Predictably, however, the Viet Cong replied two days later by blowing up a hotel being used as enlisted men's quarters in Qui Nhon, killing 23 US soldiers and wounding many more.

The next day Operation *Flaming Dart II* began when 99 strike aircraft launched from the three aircraft carriers in the South China Sea. Their targets were the barracks at Vit Thu Lu and Chanh Hoa.

The weather – at the height of the monsoon season – was atrocious but the Navy aircraft roared into the attack at Chanh Hoa despite 500ft ceilings and visibility less than one mile. Three aircraft were shot down with one pilot captured and the other two rescued. The North Vietnamese were unimpressed by the raids and continued their attacks.

## *Market Time*

February 1965 also saw the start of another Navy operation. *Market Time* was a surface and air patrol effort to reduce the seaborne infiltration into South Vietnam of communist arms and supplies. The enemy supply effort was directed by North Vietnamese Naval Transportation Group 125, which used steel-hulled, 100-ton trawlers and seagoing junks to bring the supplies direct to the Viet Cong waiting on the beaches, or to transfer their loads onto smaller junks, sampans and other craft.

The coastal surveillance operation covered the 1,200-mile South Vietnamese coast from the 17th Parallel to the Cambodian border and extended 40 miles out to sea.

American aircraft operating from ships offshore and from bases in South Vietnam, Thailand and the Philippines carried out air search of the *Market Time* area and for a brief time in 1965, Skyraiders based on

*“Capt Hayden J Lockhart became the first USAF pilot to be captured by the North Vietnamese”*

**The composition of a carrier air wing depended on its area of operations and the size of the carrier. Here, Skyraiders, Skyhawks and Phantoms crowd the deck of the USS *Coral Sea*. The Skyraiders are from Navy Attack Squadron VA-25**

aircraft carriers flew surveillance missions along the coast. Their mission was shared and then taken over by a patrol squadron based at Sangley Point in the Philippines equipped with the advanced P-3 Orion aircraft. Throughout this time up to seven SP-2H Neptune aircraft were also stationed at Tan Son Nhut and made regular patrols up and down the coast.

In addition, from May 1965 ageing Martin SP-5 Marlin seaplanes operated from tenders *Currituck* and *Salisbury Sound* anchored at Condore and Cham Islands or at Cam Ranh Bay.

When the seaplanes were withdrawn early in 1967, a squadron of 12 Neptunes were stationed ashore at Cam Ranh Bay and a detachment of P-3s began coverage of the Gulf of Siam from U Tapao RTAFB in Thailand.

In addition to seeking out communist supply vessels, the patrol aircraft were also used to shadow Russian and Chinese ships and to keep watch for any enemy torpedo boats or aircraft that might pose a threat to US ships in the Gulf of Tonkin.

## Jet bomber ops

As the plans were being made for the first *Market Time* missions, authority was finally given to use the B-57 Canberras on combat sorties and without the need to have a VNAF crewman on board. Technically, it was a violation of the 1954 Geneva Agreement, but the USA and South Vietnam felt that, since the North Vietnamese had violated the agreement, then they could too.

At 14.30 on February 19, the first of 18 B-57s from the 8th and 13th Bomb Squadrons took off from Bien Hoa. Twenty minutes later they were over the target, a suspected Viet Cong concentration near Binh Gia, about 30 miles east of Saigon, and the scene of the heavy fighting two months previously.

As the crews completed their bomb-runs, a number of secondary explosions were noted, indicating that fuel or ammunition caches had also been hit. All aircraft returned home safely as Super Sabres carried on the attack. Two days later the B-57s and F-100s were scrambled to assist a US Army Special Forces team and a CIDG (Civilian Irregular Defense Group) company that had been ambushed at the Mang Yang Pass on Route 19, east of Pleiku. The close air support prevented the enemy from overrunning the Allied forces while US helicopters moved in and evacuated the 220 men who might otherwise have been lost.

Back in Washington, officials no longer talked about withdrawing US advisers from South Vietnam, rather they recommended the deployment of additional US forces. Soon, two B-52 Stratofortress squadrons belonging to the Strategic Air Command were on their way to Anderson AFB on Guam for possible use over South Vietnam and nine more USAF Tactical Fighter Squadrons were alerted for deployment. A fourth aircraft carrier was also despatched to the South China Sea and on February 13 President Johnson approved the inauguration of an air warfare campaign against North Vietnam.

**The 20th Helicopter Squadron, later Special Operations Squadron, arrived in 1965 with its Sikorsky CH-3C helicopters. Their mission, known as *Pony Express*, was the covert transportation of indigenous soldiers and material across the Laotian and North Vietnamese borders**
*(Doug Armstrong via Phil Chinnery)*

An airborne early warning version of the Skyraider prepares for launch from the steam catapult of this carrier in the South China Sea

◀ An A-4 'Scooter' from Navy Attack Squadron VA-23 from the USS Oriskany releasing its 500lb bombs over a target near the coast in North Vietnam

▶ During the early years of the Vietnam War the Crusader was the principal US Navy fighter aircraft and the type is credited with the destruction of 18 North Vietnamese fighters

In Laos, the joint US Navy and USAF *Barrel Roll* force was redirected toward key transport bottlenecks or 'choke' points on the Ho Chi Minh Trail. The first such attack was carried out on February 28 when Skyraiders and Skyhawks from the USS *Coral Sea* attacked the road through the Mu Gia Pass near the border of North Vietnam and Laos. Although the supply route was repeatedly cut at critical points, the North Vietnamese soon managed to repair the roads, construct bypasses and maintain the logistical flow. It was obvious stronger action was needed.

## Rolling Thunder

The main attack on the North was not to be a short sharp campaign using strength and surprise, but rather a slow gradual programme of attacks, increasing in intensity over the months with the aim of persuading Hanoi to negotiate an end to its insurgency in the South.

The campaign was to be known as *Rolling Thunder* and would continue, with various pauses, for the next four years. The first *Rolling Thunder* strike took place on March 2 against the Xom Bong ammunition dump and the small naval base at Quang Khe. The attacking force consisted of 44 F-105 Thunderchiefs, 40 F-100 Super Sabres, 20 B-57 Canberras – plus seven RF-101C Voodoos to take post-strike photographs of the bomb damage. They were accompanied by a nominal VNAF force of 19 aircraft.

Three of the F-105s and two F-100s were shot down by enemy ground fire and Capt Hayden J Lockhart became the first USAF pilot to be captured by the North Vietnamese.

## Wading ashore

Less than a week later, at 09.00hrs on March 8, the 3,500 men of the 9th Marine Expeditionary Force waded ashore at Da Nang to be greeted by garland-carrying Vietnamese girls. They were the first US combat unit to deploy to South Vietnam and within a month they began to engage Viet Cong and North Vietnamese forces in combat.

A second USAF *Rolling Thunder* strike took place on March 15 and three days later the Navy joined in with aircraft from the USS *Hancock* and *Coral Sea* bombing supply buildings at Phu Van and Vinh Son.

Target allocation remained slow and strictly controlled by Washington, who even decided the timing of the raids, how many aircraft would be used and with which armament – decisions which should have been made by the experienced USAF and Navy commanders in the theatre of operations.

In an attempt to define a strategy for crippling the war-making capability of North Vietnam, the JCS submitted a four-phase programme to Secretary of Defense McNamara, incorporating the destruction of the southern part of the rail system. The idea was to isolate the North from external sources of resupply and then to destroy its internal military and industrial capability.

## Bridge busters

President Johnson and his advisers would not approve the 13-week bombing programme but they did authorise a campaign against the southern rail network.

The first on the list of targets was the Thanh Hóa railroad and highway bridge, known to the Vietnamese as Hàm Rồng (the Dragon's Jaw). The first raid took place on April 3 and involved 79 aircraft: 46 F-105s Thunderchiefs, 21 F-100 Super Sabres, two RF-101 Voodoos and ten Boeing KC-135 tankers.

Sixteen of the 46 F-105s were loaded with a pair of Bullpup missiles and each of the remaining jets carried eight 750lb bombs. The aircraft that carried the missiles and half of the bombers were scheduled to strike the bridge; the remaining 15 would provide flak suppression. Seven of the F-100s were also assigned to flak suppression, two to weather reconnaissance, four to provide CAP (Combat Air Patrol) and eight to be used for rescue top cover (RESCAP) if required.

The RESCAP and flak suppression F-100s each carried two pods of 19 2.75in rockets and the latter also had two 750lb bombs for good measure. The CAP F-100s were armed with Sidewinder missiles and the whole force of fighters was equipped

From May 1965 ageing Martin SP-5 Marlin seaplanes operated from the seaplane tenders *Currituck* and *Salisbury Sound* anchored at Condore and Cham Islands or at Cam Ranh Bay

Medevac Hueys used the callsign ‘Dustoff’ and would be vectored to the pick up area by smoke grenades ignited on the ground. Occasionally the enemy would also set off a smoke grenade to entice the pilot to land in their area, so the pilot would usually verify the colour of the smoke with the men on the ground before attempting a pick up

North Vietnamese Air Force MiG-17 pilots walk by their aircraft for a propaganda photograph *(USAF Museum)*

Photograph of SA-2 site in North Vietnam taken by a US reconnaissance aircraft in August 1965 *(USAF Museum)*

with 20mm cannons. The F-100s flew up the coast from South Vietnam while the F-105s from Thailand refuelled in the air over the Mekong River.

Post-strike photography confirmed that the bridge had taken numerous hits from the 32 missiles and 120 bombs, but only the roadway on the south side had incurred significant damage. The lack of success was no reflection on the pilots because the bridge had been grossly overbuilt. Heavy weapons would have to be dropped along the middle 12ft of the bridge to make it fall and although such accurate weapons were not available until May 1972, the Air Force prepared to strike the bridge again the following day.

This time it was attacked by 48 F-105s, each carrying eight 750lb bombs. Three hundred bombs hit the target and the bridge was severely damaged. However, the bombs were just not powerful enough and within a month the rail line was in use again.

Three F-105s were lost that day; two were shot down by four MiG-17 *Frescos* that came out of the clouds with their cannons blazing and continued out of the area at maximum speed. The Thunderchiefs were the first USAF aircraft to fall to enemy MiGs. The third F-105 was hit by anti-aircraft fire and Capt ‘Smitty’ Harris bailed out to face seven years in a prisoner of war camp. The ‘Thud’ was prone to a loss of control when the hydraulic system took even the smallest of hits and a simple back-up system could have given many pilots the chance to head for a safer bail-out area. Such a modification finally came through, but it was too late for many brave pilots.

## Airborne Early Warning

The loss of the two F-105s to the MiG-17s was of concern to the USAF. The Russian-built jets had obviously been vectored to the ‘Thuds’ by a ground controlled intercept (GCI) radar unit so, in order to provide advance warning of such attacks in future, a detachment of Lockheed EC-121D Constellations from the 552nd Airborne Early Warning and Control Wing (AEWCW) was sent to Tan Son Nhut AB.

The Connies of the *Big Eye* (later *College Eye*) task force were equipped with search radar and radio relay transmitters and soon began to fly orbits over the Gulf of Tonkin and Laos, providing radar coverage over North Vietnam and Laos. They could determine the range and altitude of hostile aircraft and issue advance warnings to friendly aircraft.

The effectiveness of MiG CAP flights was also increased by the arrival in Thailand of the first USAF F-4C Phantoms. The 18 aircraft from the 45th TFS of the 15th TFW left MacDill AFB in Florida on April 4 and flew to the RTAFB at Ubon.

The two-seat Phantoms carried a less-experienced pilot in the rear seat to operate the radar. Officially known as the pilot systems operator (PSO) – later altered to weapons system operator (WSO) when the flying requirement was dropped – the crewmember was more normally referred to as the GIB or guy in back. Although the F-4C carried air-to-air missiles and, later on, detachable gun pods, at this time it was not armed with guns. Putting it at a distinct disadvantage when it came to engage in dogfights with the enemy MiGs.

## Relaxing policies

Following a fact-finding mission to the region by Army Chief of Staff General Harold Johnson, the President relaxed some of the bombing restrictions. Targets were now selected in weekly packages with the timing of the attacks left to the local commander. Armed reconnaissance missions to hunt for targets of opportunity were allowed and flak-suppression and combat air patrol aircraft were now permitted to attack other targets on the way home from the target area.

Meanwhile, over the border in Laos, Operation *Steel Tiger* began in April as a day and night air campaign against enemy troops and supply vehicles in the southern panhandle of Laos. Both Navy and USAF aircraft were used during the daytime, but the night intruder missions were flown exclusively by USAF B-57 Canberras.

The first of these launched the campaign on April 1 when two B-57s joined a *Blind Bat* C-130 Hercules flare-ship in the area of Tchepone, where the supply routes filtered in from North Vietnam. By the end of the

**“ As the ground forces increased, so did US air power ”**

An F-100 dropping napalm on a Viet Cong position

A Martin B-57 Canberra releasing its bomb load over a target in South Vietnam

The Royal Australian Air Force's 2 Sqn flew the Canberra with great distinction in Vietnam *(USAF Museum)*

night the B-57s had destroyed a ferryboat with four trucks on it, one bridge and 20 buildings by secondary explosions (caused by exploding ammunition or fuel).

A detachment of Douglas EF-10B Skyknight aircraft from Marine Composite Reconnaissance Squadron VMCJ-1 arrived at Da Nang on April 10. They began to accompany the night bombers on their missions, to jam radar controlled anti-aircraft weapons and detect hot missile sites that might be preparing to launch. The ageing Skynights continued to fly electronic-warfare missions over Laos and North Vietnam until 1969, when they were replaced by the Grumman EA-6A Intruder.

The day after the first EF-10s flew into Da Nang, the first USMC F-4B Phantoms arrived. They were from Fighter Attack Squadron VMFA-531 from Atsugi in Japan and carried out their first combat mission the next day. Armed with air-to-air missiles and up to 16,000lbs of ordnance including bombs, Bullpup air-to-surface missiles and folding-fin rockets the Marines' Phantoms commenced their duties as close-support aircraft for combat troops on the ground.

## Searching for SAMs

The US Military Assistance Command, Vietnam (USMACV) commander, General Westmoreland, was so impressed with the Navy's support that he asked for an aircraft carrier to be permanently stationed off South Vietnam. Consequently, the Dixie Station area was established and Navy carrier aircraft began to fly regular combat missions in-country in May 1965. They continued in this role until mid-1966 when land-based aircraft were well enough established to handle most of the required air support in the South. By June 1965 five aircraft carriers were on line flying dozens of missions daily as a part of Rolling Thunder.

It was a US Navy RF-8A Crusader from the USS Coral Sea that brought back aerial photographs of the first North Vietnamese surface-to-air missile (SAM) site. The missiles were 15 miles southeast of Hanoi and the discovery led the commander of Task Force 77 on Yankee Station to fly to Saigon to discuss the new development with the commander of the Seventh Air Force. Both men recommended an immediate strike against the site but permission was refused. More sites were established over the coming months, but six months elapsed before the first SAM site was destroyed. In the meantime, both Navy and USAF aircraft and crews had been lost to the new SA-2 *Guideline* missile.

The first six Douglas RB-66C Destroyer aircraft arrived in April 1965 to take over the Early Warning, Intelligence gathering and ECM duties over North Vietnam. They were from the 41st Tactical Reconnaissance Squadron (TRS) and were joined in October by five more from the 6,460th TRS.

Another type new to the theatre was the Lockheed F-104 Starfighter – the first 24 of which arrived with the 476th TFS in Taiwan and Da Dang in April. By the end of 1967 fourteen Starfighters had been lost including two that suffered a mid-air collision over South Vietnam in September 1965.

The USAF also activated four O-1 Bird Dog squadrons in South Vietnam during April and reinforced the F-105 units in Thailand with the 563rd TFS and 421st TFS both of which had 18 aircraft each.

By mid-1965, despite the poor weather in the monsoon season, US Navy and USAF pilots were flying over 1,000 Steel Tiger sorties each month. South Vietnamese ground reconnaissance teams, led by US Green Berets, were also operating in the border areas to try to pinpoint enemy traffic on the Ho Chi Minh trail and were soon directing strikes against truck parks and supply dumps normally concealed from the air by the jungle growth or bad weather.

In order to provide a faster response against fleeting targets, the USAF began to place F-105 *Whiplash* flights on standby alert at some of the bases in Thailand. However, despite all this effort, by the end of the year the North Vietnamese were infiltrating over 4,500 men and 300 tons of supplies into South Vietnam every month.

An F-100 Super Sabre performing road convoy escort duty

The first *Rolling Thunder* strike was against targets 35 miles north of the DMZ and three F-105s and two F-100s were shot down *(USAF Museum)*

By the end of 1967 fourteen Starfighters had been lost including two that suffered a mid-air collision over South Vietnam in September 1965

## Increased manpower

The first US Army combat unit to arrive in Vietnam was the 173rd Airborne Brigade, which took up residency in Bien Hoa on May 4, 1965. During May the number of US servicemen in the country grew to over 50,000 (including 10,000 from the USAF) and two months later, on July 25, the President approved an increase in troop-levels to 125,000 men. And as the ground forces increased, so did US air power.

On May 3, Marine Observation Squadron VMO-2 flew six new UH-1E armed helicopters into Da Nang and began to take over the role of escorting Marine H-34 troop-carrying helicopters from the Army. The UH-1Es were armed with TK-2 Ground Fire Suppression Armament Kits consisting of an electrically fired M-60C machine gun on each side of the helicopter and two 2.75in rocket pods.

The USMC, whose Phantoms were now flying combat missions out of Da Nang, decided to bring in additional ground support aircraft in the shape of the Douglas A-4E Skyhawk. Since only Da Nang, Bien Hoa and Tan Son Nhut were capable of taking jets at that time, the Marines decided to build a dedicated attack aircraft facility of their own. On May 7, around 1,400 more Marines and Navy Seabees waded ashore at Chu Lai, 50 miles south of Da Nang and began to build an airfield.

Using aluminium matting, a 1,200m long Short Airfield for Tactical Support (SATS) was quickly put into place and mobile arresting gear was set up to facilitate use of the tail-hook capability of the Skyhawk. By June 1 Marine Attack Squadrons VMA-225 and 311 had arrived and within hours Skyhawks from VMA-225 had flown their first combat mission, leaving the airfield with the aid of Jet-Assisted Take-Off (JATO) equipment as the field was without an aircraft carrier-type catapult system until 1967.

## Bring on the BUFF

Following an attempt in April to destroy the Viet Cong military headquarters complex at Black Virgin Mountain – when 443 sorties were flown by single-engined bombers – the US Secretary of Defense approved General Westmoreland's request to use of the giant Boeing B-52 Stratofortress bombers. The BUFF (Big Ugly Fat 'Fella') was capable of carpet-bombing a wide area and it was hoped this would be better suited for some targets in the North.

The USAF flew its first B-52 strike of Operation *Arc Light* on June 18 against a suspected Viet Cong base in Binh Duong province, north of Saigon. Sadly, this first mission suffered a tragedy when two of the B-52s collided en-route during aerial refuelling. Eight of the twelve crewmen lost their lives as the aircraft plunged in flames into the Pacific.

Later, the three Army Special Forces bomb damage assessment teams sent into the area found little target damage before enemy snipers drove them out of the area. The USAF chiefs were satisfied with the results though and by the end of the year the B-52s were flying 300 sorties each month.

On the same day that the first B-52 mission occurred, the ARVN military took over from the government again. This time Major General Nguyen Van Thieu was installed as President and Nguyen Cao Ky, the VNAF commander, became Premier.

## MiG kill

On June 17 the US Navy scored the first MiG kill of the war when two F-4B Phantoms from VF-21 found themselves closing on a flight of four MiG-17s south of Hanoi. The Phantoms fired their Sparrow missiles and were delighted to see two of the MiGs go down in flames. Three days later, a propeller-driven A-1H Skyraider from VA-25 brought down a third MiG-17 by using its superior turning ability to out-manoeuvre the enemy jet. It was quite an accomplishment, especially as the MiG-17s were usually armed with three 23mm cannon and two underwing packs of eight 55mm air-to-air rockets.

**"A Skyraider from VA-25 brought down a MiG-17 by using its superior turning ability"**

North Vietnamese workers smile for the camera as they salvage equipment from the Thanh Hóa railroad station following a bombing raid

A Marine Skyhawk from VMA-311 taxying at Chu Lai. JATO bottles were used to launch the aircraft until an aircraft-carrier style catapult was installed in 1967

As well as flying MiG-CAP roles the F-4B Phantoms from the US Navy's VF-21 also found themselves in use for ground attack missions

By now the communists were capable of mounting regimental-size operations in many parts of South Vietnam and battalion-sized operations almost anywhere. The Viet Cong units were now equipped with modern Chinese and Soviet weapons and were being supplemented by the arrival of North Vietnamese Army regular troops. The South Vietnamese armed forces had been doing badly and it appeared that the war on the ground might be lost before the war in the air had even started. Consequently, Washington decided to commit American combat troops to battle.

## Antipodean assistance

During July, US Army Vietnam headquarters was formed at Long Binh near Saigon to support Army operations in Vietnam. The 1st Infantry Division's 2nd Brigade arrived for combat operations in III Corps and 1st Brigade, 101st Airborne Division arrived for combat in II Corps.

The 1st Battalion, Royal Australian Regiment had already arrived in III Corps and they were soon joined by a New Zealand Army field artillery battery. They were the first Allied combat units to arrive, but Thai and Korean combat troops were on the way and soon Royal Australian Air Force (RAAF) Canberra bombers, Caribou transports and UH-1 helicopters would also deploy.

As overall ground commander, General Westmoreland had to decide how to use his combat troops to best effect. He did not, and never would have, enough men nor the time, to seize and hold areas of the countryside in order to destroy the Viet Cong infrastructure and pacify the villages. Even at the height of American involvement when over half a million servicemen were in Vietnam, only 80,000 were combat troops, the rest being support and service personnel.

'Search and Destroy' became the name of the game and the US troops were sent out into the countryside to locate the enemy and then destroy him using the superior US firepower. It may have been a good theory at the time, but whereas the North Vietnamese leaders had an unlimited supply of 'cannon fodder' to fill their fighting units, the USA did not. At this stage of the war it was not a problem but later, when the US media began to show the war in all its questionable glory and the number of coffins arriving at Stateside airports turned from a trickle to a flood, the American public would demand the return of its sons.

## Flight of the Intruder

Meanwhile, the war in the air continued with the arrival on Yankee Station in July of the aircraft carrier USS *Independence*. One of the squadrons on board was VA-75, the 'Sunday Punchers', who were equipped with the new Grumman A-6A Intruder. The Intruders' primary missions were all weather and night attacks and the aircraft could accurately drop its 15,000lbs of bombs in all weathers thanks to its DIANE weapons delivery system. Later in the war KA-6s would be used as airborne fuel tankers and EA-6s on electronic warfare missions, including radar destruction or suppression.

July also saw the USAF achieve its first MiG kill – almost a full month behind its Navy colleagues. On July 10, a flight of four F-4C Phantoms from the 45th TFS at Ubon decided to try a new tactic while escorting some F-105s on a strike mission. As the 'Thuds' began their bombing runs, the Phantoms held back and waited for the enemy to appear, as they usually did, when the strike force was most vulnerable. Suddenly, they sighted a flight of MiG-17s and rolled into the attack, despatching two of the enemy with their Sidewinder missiles.

However, the dogfight highlighted a problem that would plague the Phantom crews throughout the war: inadequate fuel capacity. In this case it caused the two MiG-killers to land at Udorn, which was closer than Ubon.

Two weeks later a SAM missile exploded in the middle of a flight of four F-4Cs from the 47th TFS, destroying one and damaging three others. By the end of the year 180 SAM launches had been recorded, resulting in the loss of four more USAF and six US Navy/Marine Corps aircraft.

**The Grumman A-6A Intruder could bomb accurately in all weathers with its DIANE weapons delivery system and it could carry up to 15,000lbs of bombs, second only to the B-52. Here a pair of Intruders flying off the USS *Constellation* release their prodigious bomb loads over an enemy target**

**In order to provide escorts for the rescue helicopters over Laos and North Vietnam the A-1Es of the 602nd Air Commando Squadron were moved into Udorn in August. Here an HH-3E from the 37th ARRS is escorted by two 'Sandy' A-1s from the 6th SOS**

**The 1st Cavalry Division (Airmobile) began to arrive at An Khe at the end of August. They brought with them over 400 helicopters including the twin rotor CH-47A Chinooks which could carry troops or freight**

No doubt to the relief of the pilots, an adequate Search and Rescue force was now in place. Three Douglas SC-54 'Rescuemasters' had arrived at Udorn to operate as airborne command posts until the first HC-130s arrived in December 1965. They replaced the ageing HU-16 Albatross amphibians, which then moved to Da Nang and spent the next two years flying rescue missions in the Gulf of Tonkin.

The HH-43B/F helicopters were also joined in July by two Sikorsky CH-3Cs on loan from Tactical Air Command. With their extra capacity, longer range and protective armour, they helped to bridge the SAR gap until the first purpose-built HH-3E Jolly Green Giants arrived in December.

Pilots ejecting 'feet wet' over the Gulf of Tonkin could count on rescue by the Navy's SH-3 and UH-2 helicopters. The Sikorsky SH-3A Sea Kings came from the anti-submarine squadrons aboard the carriers and the smaller Kaman UH-2A/B Seasprites from detachments of the Helicopter Combat Support Squadrons on the carriers and smaller ships of Task Force 77.

## Marine Corps victory

On August 11 the USS *Princeton* sailed from Long Beach, California with Marine Air Group (MAG) 36 on board. The Group comprised three UH-34 squadrons with 24 helicopters each plus VMO-6 with 27 UH-1Es and six Sikorsky H-37 Deuces from Heavy Transport Squadron HMH-462. They were bound for Ky Ha, north of Chu Lai and their first task on arrival was to build themselves a helicopter base.

MAG-16 had already moved its three UH-34 squadrons and elements of VMO-2 into the Marble Mountain air facility near Da Nang but as soon as MAG-36 arrived, the monsoon rains began and turned the area into a sea of mud.

While the build-up was underway the Viet Cong moved the 3,000 men of its 1st Regiment close to Chu Lai, ready to try to overrun the airfield. The Marines decided to pre-empt the attack and on August 18 they launched three Marine infantry battalions against the Viet Cong. Operation *Starlight* lasted four days, with Phantoms and Skyhawks flying support missions so close to the base that they were releasing their bombs even before they had time to raise their wheels. Fifty Marines were killed, but the Viet Cong lost over 600 in their first major defeat at the hands of the Americans. Two months later, the Viet Cong attacked the helicopter base at Marble Mountain, destroying 19 UH-1Es and UH-34s and badly damaging eleven others.

August would also see the activation of the 1st Cavalry Division (Airmobile). The Airmobile Division concept combined the resources of the 11th Air Assault Division and the 2nd Infantry Division; namely 1,600 vehicles, 15,800 men and 434 helicopters and aircraft and the advance party arrived at An Khe at the end of the month and began to clear the 'golf course', which was to become the world's largest helipad. The unit's helicopters were capable of performing troop-lift, gunship support, aerial rocket artillery, medevac, artillery spotting, liaison and air cavalry reconnaissance missions.

The troop-lift role was carried out by

Men of B Troop, 1st Squadron, 9th Cavalry are landed by a 'slick' troopship during a mission. The trooper nearest has a grenade launcher attached to his M-16 rifle and carries extra ammunition belts for the squad machine gun

A Northrop F-5A Freedom Fighter of the Vietnamese Air Force. They could only carry a small payload but were relatively easy to maintain

Wild Weasel F-105F Thunderchiefs equipped with *Shrike* missiles en-route to a North Vietnamese SAM site

An impressive display of a Spooky's nocturnal firepower. The AC-47s were designed to provide fire support at night for isolated outposts such as Special Forces camps. They were each equipped with three miniguns based on the renowned Gatling design, with each gun capable of firing 6,000 rounds per minute

the 13-troop-carrying UH-1D; fire-power was supplied by the UH-1B gunships; CH-47A Chinooks could carry troops or freight; CH-54 Tarhe flying cranes were used to haul artillery pieces and recover downed aircraft and the OH-13 was used for observation and reconnaissance duties.

By October the communists had begun a concerted effort to cut South Vietnam in two. The programme began with a ten-day attack by 2,200 North Vietnamese Army (NVA) troops on the Plei Me Special Forces camp from October 18. The USAF dropped more than 1,500,000lbs of bombs on the attackers before they broke off the attack. The 1st Cavalry Division was then called in to find the retreating enemy (and their reinforcements); the subsequent Operation *Silver Bayonet* lasted a month and became known as the Battle of the Ia Drang Valley. Around 1,800 NVA troops were killed for the loss of 240 Americans.

## *Wild Weasels*

Additional fighter squadrons arrived during October when the first of five more F-100 squadrons took up residence at Bien Hoa and Da Nang. McDonnell Douglas RF-4C reconnaissance Phantoms also arrived from the 16th TRS at Shaw AFB and moved into the already crowded Tan Son Nhut Air Base.

On October 23, the 450th TFS flew the first dozen Northrop F-5A Freedom Fighters into South Vietnam. They were a part of the *Skoshi Tiger* evaluation programme and although they could only carry a small payload, they were relatively easy to maintain and repair. The USAF began to train VNAF pilots on the type in Arizona and in 1967 the F-5s were turned over to the VNAF.

As losses to SAM missiles began to mount, the USAF tried to counter the threat by launching *Iron Hand* F-105D SAM suppression flights against their launch sites. This dangerous job became easier with the arrival in November of the 388th TFW's first two-seater F-100F Wild Weasel aircraft. They were based at the RTAFB at Korat and were equipped with radar homing and warning (RHAW) sets which enabled them to home in on the SA-2 missile's Fansong radar guidance signals.

Once the SAM site was discovered, the F-100 would mark the target with rockets then let the bomb-carrying F-105s destroy them. The F-100Fs could also give early warning of an impending SAM firing, thus allowing the aircraft in the area to take evasive action.

However, the F-100s were much slower than the 'Thuds' and the following year they would be phased out in favour of RHAW-equipped F-105 Wild Weasels.

## Puff the Magic Dragon

Late November saw the arrival in theatre of the first Douglas AC-47 gunships. Allocated to the 4th Air Commando Squadron at Tan Son Nhut they flew their first operational sortie on December 15. The AC-47s were designed to provide fire support at night for isolated outposts such as Special Forces camps and were equipped with three Gatling miniguns. Each of the three guns was capable of firing 6,000 rounds per minute and the aircraft was modified to carry 24,000 rounds of ammunition as well 45 200,000-candlepower flares. Although its operational callsign was Spooky, those who had witnessed one of its nocturnal displays dubbed it the Puff the Magic Dragon.

Towards the end of November the USAF also began to camouflage its aircraft – with the exception of the O-1 FACs who needed to be seen from the air against the jungle background. Shortly afterwards a system was begun of allocating two letter tail codes to the aircraft according to where they were based.

## Enter the *Enterprise*

The US Navy's first nuclear-powered aircraft carrier USS *Enterprise* arrived on Yankee Station on December 2 with Air Wing 9 on board. The wing consisted of four A-4C Skyhawk squadrons, two F-4B Phantom squadrons, an RA-5C Vigilante squadron

## MEDAL OF HONOR

Bruce Crandall – November 14, 1965
Ed Freeman – November 14, 1965
Major Bruce Crandall's Medal of Honor was the (joint) earliest in the Vietnam War – although it was not actually awarded until 2007. He received the award for repeatedly flying his UH-1 into a landing zone under intense enemy fire to rescue and resupply troops.

On November 14, 1965, while assigned to A Company, 229th Assault Helicopter Battalion, 1st Air Cavalry Division, Major Crandall led the first major division operation of the Vietnam War, landing elements of the 1st Battalion and 2nd Battalion of the 7th Cavalry Regiment, and the 5th Cavalry Regiment, into Landing Zone X-Ray in the Ia Drang Valley. During the fierce battle that followed, he and wingman Ed Freeman performed 14 flights – 12 of which were made after the Medical Evacuation unit refused to land in the intensely 'hot' landing zone. Crandall's helicopters evacuated more than 75 casualties during a 16-hour flight day that started at 06.00hrs. The two also flew in the ammunition needed for the 7th Cavalry to survive. By the end of the war Crandall had flown over 900 combat missions. He was initially awarded the Distinguished Flying Cross but on February 26, 2007 this was upgraded to the Medal of Honor, awarded by President George W Bush.

Captain Ed Freeman had fought in both World War Two and the Korean War and was 38 years old when he took part in the same battle as Major Crandall. By the time he landed his heavily damaged Huey at the end of the day, he had landed in the hot LZ 14 times and had been wounded four times. He was subsequently promoted to Major and went home from Vietnam in 1966 and retired in 1967. Freeman's commanding officer nominated him for the Medal of Honor, but not in time to meet a two-year deadline then in place. The two-year rule was removed in 1995 and he was formally presented with the medal on July 16, 2001 by President George W Bush.

**This Douglas EKA-3B Skywarrior is unfolding its wings and vertical stabiliser prior to take-off from the USS *Bon Homme Richard*. The type was used for airborne refuelling of Navy fighters.**

and one of KA-3B Skywarriors for airborne refuelling.

There were also detachments of E-1B Tracers for the airborne early warning role; UH-2 Seasprite helicopters for SAR and utility duties; EA-3B Skywarriors for electronic intelligence gathering and RA-3Bs for reconnaissance.

With separate command and control organisations involved in the planning of Navy and Air Force *Rolling Thunder* missions against North Vietnam, it was decided to divide the North into six areas or route packages. In general, the USAF would attack inland targets while the shorter-range Navy aircraft concentrated on those near the coast.

The Johnson administration also imposed a 30-mile radius restricted zone and a ten-mile prohibited zone around Hanoi and similar zones of four and ten miles around Haiphong. This was coupled with a 30-mile buffer zone along the border with China. Permission to strike any of the important targets in these zones had to be obtained from Washington and this was seldom given. F-105 pilots could clearly see the enemy MiGs taking off from Phuc Yen airfield, near Hanoi, but were forbidden to engage them.

However, as the year came to an end, authority was given for a strike against one target only within the restricted area of Haiphong. On December 22 a group of 100 aircraft from the USS *Enterprise*, *Kitty Hawk* and *Ticonderoga* hit the power station at Uong Bi, 15 miles northeast of the harbour city of Haiphong. It was the first raid on an industrial target, as opposed to bases and support installations and all sections of the complex were hit for the loss of two Skyhawks.

Two days later President Johnson ordered a Christmas truce and the bombing ceased for 37 days. While Washington waited in vain for the communists to talk peace, North Vietnam took advantage of the bombing halt to improve its anti-aircraft defences and disperse its petroleum and lubricants facilities. The first phase of *Rolling Thunder* had clearly been a failure. In the 16 months since August 1964, nearly 57,000 combat sorties had been flown from the ten aircraft carriers and over 100 aircraft had been lost. A total of 82 men had been killed, captured or were missing and 46 others had been rescued.

**The USAF flew its first B-52 strike of Operation Arc Light on June 18, 1965 against a suspected Viet Cong base in Binh Duong**

Army troops disembarking from a CH-47A Chinook during Operation *Masher*

# BIG BELLY BUFFS, CHINOOK GUNSHIPS AND *FISHBED* KILLERS

## The peak years of the war in South East Asia began in 1966 – from which point the US Armed Forces found themselves fighting not one war but three

Throughout 1966 the *Rolling Thunder* bombing campaign continued over North Vietnam in the vain hope of persuading the North Vietnamese to discuss peace.

USAF and US Navy aircraft flew north daily, but the restrictions imposed by the Johnson administration, together with the most powerful air defence system in the world, prevented a successful conclusion to the campaign.

Meanwhile, in South Vietnam the ARVN troops took a back seat while American combat troops sought to bring Viet Cong and North Vietnamese Army (NVA) units to battle. Employing the mobility afforded by the Bell UH-1 helicopter, the Americans launched search and destroy operations to pin down the enemy and use their massive firepower and air support to destroy them. But after the loss of 4,000 helicopters and 58,000 men, it became clear that while North Vietnam was apparently prepared to continue fighting forever, the American public was not. No doubt the 'folks back home' would have been equally concerned to discover that their sons and husbands were fighting a secret, undeclared air war over the border in Laos as well.

While Operation *Barrel Roll* continued to hit targets in the northeast of the country, the *Steel Tiger* campaign against the infiltration routes in the eastern edges of the southern panhandle was split into two, with operations south of the 17th Parallel and adjacent to the South Vietnamese border being renamed *Tiger Hound*. By 1966 American aircraft were flying 1,000 sorties a month in Laos, and between 1964 and 1970 they were to drop more than 2.2 million tons of bombs onto the infiltration routes of the Ho Chi Minh Trail.

### Major bases

As 1966 began, the USAF had 500 aircraft and 21,000 men at seven major bases in South Vietnam. Da Nang, Pleiku, Nha Trang, Cam Ranh Bay, Bin Thuy, Bien Hoa and Tan Son Nhut were all in use, and Phan Rang and Tuy Hoa would open later in the year and work began on Phu Cat Air Base.

In Thailand, USAF squadrons were present at Ubon, Udorn, Takhli, Korat and Don Muang. U Tapao would open later in the year while development continued at Nakhon Phanom Air Base.

Three aircraft carriers were positioned at Yankee Station with another one located further south at Dixie Station and the total number of American combat and support troops in Vietnam had risen to 181,000.

By the time the *Rolling Thunder* campaign began again on 31 January 1966, following a 37-day ceasefire, North Vietnam had built up its anti-aircraft defences to around 2,000 guns at 400 sites. These consisted mainly of 37mm and 57mm weapons, but included a few 85mm and 100mm as well. Fifty-six surface-to-air missile sites had also been pinpointed by reconnaissance flights.

During the hiatus, NVA MiG pilots had been improving their tactics, as had the SAM operators who managed to bring down an RB-66C Destroyer near Vinh in February, despite continued jamming and evasive action.

On the morning of March 8, the weary H-34 and H-37 crews at Marble Mountain looked up to see 27 Boeing-Vertol CH-46A Sea Knight helicopters flying in over the white sand of the beach. They belonged to HMM-165 and were a welcome addition to the Marines' helicopter inventory. With

Three of the four ACH-47A gunships were destroyed in two years, one in a most bizarre and tragic accident, when a mounting pin on a 20mm cannon separated during a firing run, causing the gun to elevate and destroy the forward rotor blades. All the crew were killed

a crew of three, the twin-engined assault and transport helicopter could carry up to 25 troops or 4,000lbs of cargo. They were joined three months later by HMM-265 with its 24 CH-46As. It soon became apparent, however, that the beautiful white sand of the Vietnamese lowlands was a greater hazard to the CH-46s than the Viet Cong. Sand was being sucked into the engines, requiring the powerplants to be replaced after every 300 landings; sand was also finding its way into the fuel system, causing erratic operation. Air and fuel filters were hastily fitted, as were main rotor blades with nickel-plated leading edges, which lasted ten times longer than the original stainless steel ones. It was not long before a series of fatal crashes highlighted structural defects in the CH-46, and the Sea Knight fleet was grounded more than once while modifications took place.

> "The total number of American troops in Vietnam had risen to 181,000"

## Ground war

On the ground, the troop build-up continued throughout the year, with the number of divisions increasing from three to seven and the brigades from two to four, plus an armoured cavalry regiment. The United States Marine Corps (USMC) was responsible for the northern part of South Vietnam in I Corps, the Army settled in the two middle regions of II and III Corps and the South Vietnamese took responsibility for IV Corps area in the Mekong Delta. Soon operations such as *Van Buren*, *Paul Revere* and *El Paso* II began, culminating in the multi-brigade Operation *Attleboro* in November in Tay Ninh Province, which finished with a Viet Cong and NVA 'body count' of 1,106.

On March 9, a Viet Cong force of over 2,000 men attacked the Special Forces camp at the southern end of the A Shau

On October 9, 1966 Commander Richard M Bellinger was the first Navy pilot to shoot down a MiG-21. He had himself been shot down by a MiG three months earlier over Hanoi but was rescued

An F-105 laden with six bombs and two wing drop tanks prepares to taxi to the runway for another mission over North Vietnam

**64th Fighter Interceptor Squadron Convair F-102A Delta Dagger 56-1333 returns to Da Nang in 1966 as a C-123 lands behind** *(USAF Museum)*

**▲ An F-100 from the 416thTFW looking for targets in March 1966 armed with two 500lb bombs**

**◄ A flight of 481st TFS North American F-100D Super Sabres over Vietnam in February 1966. Early F-100s were unpainted when they arrived in Southeast Asia like the foreground aircraft, but all eventually received camouflage paint like the aircraft in the background** *(USAF Museum)*

**Eight Douglas/On-Mark A-26A Invaders arrived at Nakhon Phanom in Thailand on June 9 to take part in Project *Big Eagle***

**An A-26A Invader starting its engines on the ramp at Nakhon Phanom in 1966**

Valley, near the Laotian border. Dense cloud cover prevented any air support until the following day when over 200 air strikes were made, killing at least 500 of the attackers.

During one of the air strikes, Major Wayne Myers of the 1st Air Commando Squadron crash-landed his A-1E Skyraider on the camp's badly damaged airstrip. Seeing his fellow pilot's predicament, Major Bernard C Fisher landed his own Skyraider and taxied the length of the debris-strewn runway, picked up Myers and took off again through a hail of enemy fire.

For his daring rescue Fisher was awarded the Air Force's first Medal of Honor in Southeast Asia (although others achieved in 1965 were subsequently awarded in retrospect – see page 47).

That evening the camp was abandoned and the survivors evacuated by helicopter. Two years would pass before American troops returned to retake the valley.

## Big belly BUFFs

In April, B-52D Stratofortresses with the 'Big Belly' modification began to replace the B-52Fs on Guam in the Marianas. The modification increased the internal bomb load to 60,000lbs – 22,000lbs more than the B-52F.

They flew their first mission over North Vietnam on April 11, when they struck the Mu Gia pass through which NVA troops and supplies passed on the way to the northern reaches of the Ho Chi Minh Trail. It was the largest bombing raid since World War Two and over 600 tons of bombs were dropped.

Two months later the USAF installed the Combat Skyspot ground-directed bombing system in South Vietnam. A controller in a ground radar guidance unit would direct the bombers along a designated route to a bomb drop point and signal the release of the bombs at the proper moment.

In the first air battle over North Vietnam since July 10 the previous year, USAF F-4Cs shot down two MiG-17s and engaged new MiG-21 *Fishbed* fighters for the first time on April 23. The first USAF kill of a MiG-21 was scored in a battle on April 26, when a *Fishbed* was downed by an AIM-9 Sidewinder fired by an F-4C from the 35th TFW at Da Nang.

On May 13, the 53rd Aviation Detachment, Field Evaluation (Provisional) arrived in Vietnam and joined the 147th

On the ground the troop build-up continued throughout the year, with the number of divisions increasing from three to seven and the brigades from two to four, plus an armoured cavalry regiment

USAF losses for 1966 amounted to 379 aircraft, mostly to anti-aircraft artillery and surface-to-air missiles. Here wreckage is recovered by a North Vietnamese female soldier

This F-4D from the 13th Tactical Fighter Squadron, 432nd Tactical Reconnaissance Wing is equipped with Sparrow and Sidewinder missiles

Aviation Company (Medium Helicopter) at Vung Tau. The 147th was an ACH-47A Chinook unit and had arrived in Vietnam in November 1965.

The 1st Cavalry Division's 228th Aviation Brigade had been the first Chinook unit to deploy to the theatre when it brought its CH-47 troop carrying helicopters over in September 1965 but the ACH-47A were armoured gunships, armed to the teeth with rockets, machine guns, cannons and grenade launchers.

Over the next two years, three of the four were destroyed, one in a most bizarre and tragic accident, when a mounting pin on a 20mm cannon separated during a firing run, causing the gun to elevate and destroy the forward rotor blades. All the crew were killed.

## *Carolina Moon*

On May 30, another attempt to destroy the Thanh Hóa Bridge was made using, of all things, a C-130 transport aircraft. Operation *Carolina Moon* involved new 'mass-focus' bombs, which would be dropped into the Song Ma River, float down to the bridge and detonate when sensors in the bomb detected the metal of the bridge structure. The weapons weighed 5,000lbs and resembled large 8ft-diameter pancakes.

The design was such that the weapon was detonated initially around its periphery, with the resultant force of the explosion focused along the axis of the weapon in both directions. The only problem was that, due to its size, the new weapon could only be carried by a C-130.

**The B-52 saw extensive use over North Vietnam in 1966** *(USAF Museum)*

**A USAF Douglas A-1E Skyraider drops a white phosphorus bomb on a Viet Cong position in South Vietnam in 1966** *(USAF Museum)*

**US Navy F-4B Phantoms from VMFA-115 at rest at Da Nang in 1966** *(US Navy)*

The first mission went ahead as planned and five weapons were dropped in the river one mile from the bridge. Later it was discovered that four of the five bombs had exploded, but without causing damage to the bridge. A second C-130 flew the same route the next night, but was hit by AAA fire and crashed before releasing its load. There were no survivors and the mass-focus weapon was never used again in Southeast Asia. The bridge would remain standing until laser-guided bombs reached the theatre later in the war.

## On-Mark Invaders

Eight Douglas A-26A Invaders arrived at Nakhon Phanom in Thailand on June 8 to take part in Project *Big Eagle*. They were a batch from a group of 50 B-26K modified by On-Mark Engineering and belonged to Detachment 9 of the 1st Air Commando Wing.

Equipped with 14 forward-firing 0.50in machine guns, a 5,000lb bomb load and extra fuel tanks, they began to fly hunter-killer missions against trucks on the Ho Chi Minh Trail. They replaced the earlier AC-47 Spookys and would in turn be succeeded by AC-119 and AC-130 gunships.

The month of June also saw the *Rolling Thunder* campaign extended to North Vietnam's vital petroleum storage and distribution system and by the middle of July, Navy aircraft had struck the major tank farms at Hanoi, Haiphong and Bac Giang, destroying more than half of the enemy's oil stocks.

By this time though, much of the petrol, oil and lubricant (POL) stocks had been dispersed around the countryside and US military spent the latter half of the year locating and destroying fuel-laden trucks, railroad cars, barges and smaller storage dumps. At the same time, multi-carrier strikes were aimed at devastating the critical North Vietnamese rail yards at Thanh Hóa , Phu Ly, Ninh Binh and Vinh.

By August 1966 the North Vietnamese air defence radar system consisted of 271 radars, 4,400 anti-aircraft guns and 20-25 battalions of surface-to-air missiles. Their fighter strength was around 65 aircraft including the modern MiG-21 equipped with *Atoll* air-to-air missiles. In September the MiG force went on the offensive from their five bases in the Hanoi area, which were immune to attack. Confronted by daily MiG-21 challenges, the Air Force had to divert F-4Cs from their primary strike role to exclusive aerial combat against the MiGs.

**A long line of wounded are helped aboard a Marine CH-46 Sea Knight. The type was plagued with maintenance issues and structural defects when they first arrived**

## Tragedy on the *Oriskany*

On October 26, during an intense *Rolling Thunder* period of action, the US carrier force suffered a tragic mishap. A seaman on board USS *Oriskany* improperly handled a flare, which ignited other munitions and set the forward end of the carrier ablaze. It took three hours to extinguish the fire, by which time 19 crewmen and 25 naval aviators had died. The ship left the area for repairs and was replaced by the *Coral Sea*.

By the end of the year American ground troops in the region had increased to 385,300 men; fighting together with 735,900 South Vietnamese Armed Forces and 52,500 Allied personnel. They were now confronted with an estimated enemy strength of 282,000, including 110,000 NVA regulars, who had crossed the border from the North.

Since the war had begun some 47,712 South Vietnamese and 6,644 US military personnel had been killed in action.

At this point in the war, American tactical aircraft had flown 106,500 attack sorties and B-52s had conducted another 280 over the North, dropping 165,000 tons of bombs.

USAF aircraft losses for the year came to 379 with F-105s suffering the most (126), followed by F-4s (56), A-1s (41), O-1s (37), F-100s (26), RF-101s (17) and B-57s (13). The majority of the losses were caused by anti-aircraft fire and SAMs, with only five USAF and Navy aircraft lost to MiGs throughout the year. The MiGs paid for their victories though, by losing 23 of their number to US fighters; 17 to USAF and six to Navy crews.

MiG-21 hit and run raids increased at the year's end and the first F-105 went down to an *Atoll* air-to-air missile. The USAF decided that it was time something was done about the MiGs and as 1967 began, the *Wolfpack* prepared to leave its lair. ❖

## MEDAL OF HONOR

**Bernie Fisher – March 10, 1966**

Major Bernie Fisher was awarded the Medal of Honor for landing his Douglas A-1 Skyraider on the airstrip at the besieged A Shau Valley Special Forces camp to rescue another A-1 pilot who had crash-landed on the airstrip.

In the early hours of March 10, 1966, Bernie Fisher led a flight of Skyraiders from the 1st and 602nd Air Commando Squadrons down through a gap in the clouds to give support to forces under attack from the 95th NVA Regiment. The detachment commander had asked that the camp be strafed and bombed but a barrage of anti-aircraft weapons and hundreds of automatic weapons opened fire on Skyraider and Major Wayne Myers felt his machine lurch.

He later recalled: "I've been hit by 50 calibres before, but this was something bigger, maybe the Chinese 37mm cannon. Almost immediately the engine started sputtering and cutting out and then it conked out for good. The cockpit filled with smoke. I got on the radio and gave my callsign, Surf 41, and said 'I've been hit and hit hard.' Hobo 51, that was Bernie, came right back and said, 'Roger, you're on fire and burning clear back past your tail.' I was way too low to bail out, so I told him I would have to put it down on the camp airstrip.'

As the blazing aircraft cleared the threshold, Myers realised that he was going too fast to stop and raised his landing gear for a crash landing. The belly fuel tank blew as he touched down, and a sheet of flame followed the aircraft as it skidded several hundred feet before coming to rest beside the runway. Myers climbed out of the cockpit, ran along the wing and sought shelter in the brush alongside the strip as the remaining Skyraiders made repeated strafing attacks to protect the fort and the downed airman. The Viet Cong were all around Myers, and there was no time to wait for a rescue helicopter. Fisher decided to land and pick Myers up himself:

"I turned and touched down at the end of the runway. I used all the brakes I could, but the strip was only 2,000ft [609m] long. This was the only time I was scared, because it didn't look like I was going to be able to stop. I hit the brakes as hard as I could and pulled the flaps up, which gave me a little more weight on the brakes. I think I must have been skidding on the steel planking [which] was a little bit slick from the dampness."

Fisher actually went off the end of the runway and his tail struck a 55 US Gal drum when he turned and taxied down the runway looking for Myers. He hit the brakes as he saw his friend waving vigorously and as Myers reached the aircraft Fisher pulled him headfirst on to the floor of the cockpit. "It was hard on his head, but he didn't complain," said Fisher later. By the time the Skyraider lifted off it had been hit nineteen times.

On January 19, 1967 President Johnson awarded Bernie Fisher the Medal of Honor for his actions. He was the first Air Force member to receive the medal for action in Vietnam.

Colonel Robin Olds sprays a star on his Phantom following his first MiG kill

# INTER-SERVICE RIVALRY AND A FALSE SENSE OF SECURITY

## In a year that saw the introduction of Sandy Skyraiders, Misty Super Sabres, Jolly Green Giants, Spectre gunships and Corsair IIs, the US forces enjoyed a number of major successes

On January 2, 1967, a force of 56 F-4C Phantoms from the 8th Tactical Fighter Wing (TFW)'s *Wolfpack* roared down the runway at Ubon in Thailand and set a course for North Vietnam. Operation *Bolo* had begun.

The task of the *Wolfpack*, led by the legendary Colonel Robin Olds, was to lure the enemy MiG fighters out of the sanctuary of their bases and into combat. They were accompanied by Phantoms from the 366th TFW, F-105 Thunderchiefs *Iron Hand* surface-to-air (SAM) suppression flights from the 355th and 388th TFWs as well as F-104 Starfighters, EB-66s and RC-121s, and KC-135s in the tanker role.

The *Wolfpack* Phantoms used Thunderchief callsigns, altitudes, frequencies and airspeeds to convince the North Vietnamese radar controllers that another F-105 bomber force was inbound. The ruse worked and as the MiG-21s from Phuc Yen Air Base climbed through the clouds, they ran head-on into the first flight of Phantoms, led by Olds.

During the ensuing melee, Olds found himself on the tail of a MiG and threw his Phantom into a violent barrel roll. Closing in on his target, he fired a Sidewinder missile, which veered sharply as it locked-on to the MiG, accelerated and blew it apart. Six more MiGs went down that day, followed by another pair two days later. The North Vietnamese had been taught a hard lesson and the skies remained clear of MiGs for the next couple of months.

### Inter-service rivalry

Following a long bout of inter-service rivalry, the US Army transferred all of its 97 C-7 Caribou aircraft to the USAF in January, when the Army agreed to relinquish all claims to the operation of fixed-wing tactical airlift aircraft, in return for a virtual monopoly on the use of the helicopter.

The two services had other problems to contend with. A shortage of bombs was causing aircraft to fly sorties with only a partial load of ordnance and urgent steps had to be taken to prevent a critical manpower shortage as experienced pilots came to the end of their tours of duty.

The Army was particularly hard hit and many pilots were called back for second tours in Vietnam while the training programme strained to keep up with the need for helicopter pilots.

### Holiday truce

President Johnson and his advisers insisted on a four-day truce for the Vietnamese Tet religious holiday on February 8 – despite the protestations of leaders on the ground and the Joint Chiefs of Staff (JCS).

As the truce began, the North Vietnamese started to move 34,000 tons of supplies southward. Again, the North Vietnamese were unwilling to talk peace and the JCS urged for the release of more targets in the *Rolling Thunder* restricted and prohibited areas. The President only approved a few of the targets, choosing those that offered the least risk of counter-escalation. The remaining power plants were included, except those in the centre of Hanoi and Haiphong, as were the Haiphong cement plant and the Thai Nguyen iron and steel plant. The Thai Nguyen iron and steel works was the only one in the North capable of making bridge sections, barges and POL drums and it was attacked by F-105s and by F-4Cs on March 10.

By now, new technology had provided the US strike aircraft with the electronic countermeasures (ECM) pod. This had

On April 23, 1967, pilot Capt Jerry Hoblit (left) and EWO Capt Tom Wilson flew in a four aircraft F-105 *Wild Weasel* formation on a strike against the heavily-defended area around Thai Nguyen, North Vietnam. Dodging three SA-2s, Hoblit and Wilson bombed one SAM site and fired their Shrikes against another. When an SA-2 missile damaged the lead aircraft, Hoblit and Wilson kept the SAM crew's attention by engaging it, dodging yet another SA-2. Hoblit and Wilson then remained behind to cover the crew of an RF-4C that had been shot down before the strike. None of the strike aircraft were lost. For their valour Hoblit was awarded the Air Force Cross and Wilson was awarded the Silver Star *(USAF Museum)*

During the month of May 1967 five MiG-21s were shot down over North Vietnam – including three claimed by *Wolfpack* commander Colonel Robin Olds *(USAF Museum)*

the ability to jam the enemy radar in such a way that the enemy could not determine exact aircraft range and bearing information. To gain maximum coverage from their pods, pilots had to fly a specific flight formation position both laterally and vertically. The radar jamming capabilities of the ECM pod caused the North Vietnamese to begin inaccurate barrage firing with SAMs and anti-aircraft artillery (AAA) and gave the US aircraft some freedom within the North Vietnamese SAM environment.

However, the MiGs still remained a problem and finally the restriction on attacking enemy airfields was temporarily lifted. On April 24, 1967 US Navy and USAF aircraft struck the airfields at Kep, Hoa Lac and Kien An, destroying a score of MiGs on the ground.

## Australian airpower

In the South, the Royal Australian Air Force's 2 Sqn deployed to Phan Rang AB and flew its first combat sorties on April 23.Equipped with Canberra light bombers and using the callsign Magpie, they were one of the most combat-effective units in South Vietnam and flew sorties for over three years before losing their first jet.

Elsewhere the USAF's 19th Fighter Squadron (Commando) at Bien Hoa transferred its 18 Northrop F-5A Tiger aircraft to the Vietnamese Air Force (VNAF) 522nd Fighter Squadron on April 17. By June, the first jet aircraft squadron in the VNAF was operational and the VNAF eventually possessed eight such squadrons, using F-5As, RF-5As, two-seater F-5Bs and the more powerful F-5E Tiger IIs – most of which were destined to be captured by the North Vietnamese at the end of the war.

On May 9, the vitally important power plant in the centre of Hanoi was struck, but instead of following up with similar attacks, the outcry from the North Vietnamese Government was so effective that Washington forbade further attacks within ten miles of Hanoi. The North also figured out which areas were restricted and prohibited and moved vital facilities into those areas accordingly.

Throughout the month of May, new types of aircraft and helicopters continued to arrive in South Vietnam and Thailand. The Marine Heavy Lift Squadron HMH-463 arrived at Marble Mountain with its 22 Sikorsky CH-53A Sea Stallion helicopters and these joined the four CH-53As of Detachment A, which had arrived in January.

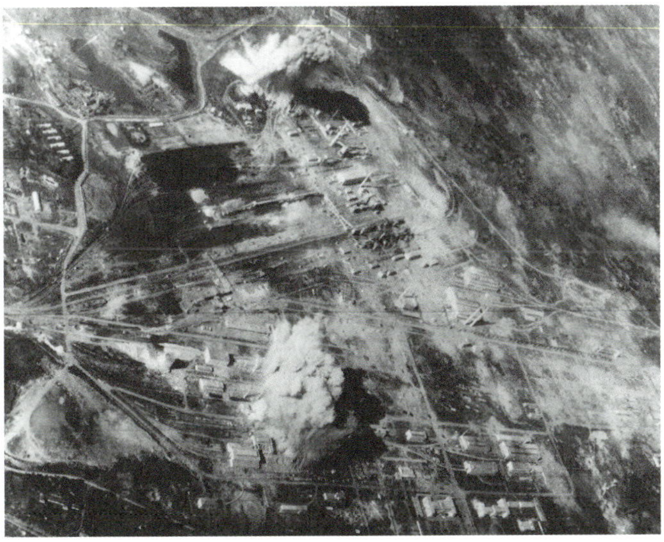

The Thai Nguyen iron and steel works was the only one in the North capable of making bridge sections, barges and oil drums. It was attacked by F-105s and by F-4Cs on March 10 and again on April 23, when this photograph was taken

A CH-53A Sea Stallion lifts a 105mm howitzer into position on a Marine fire support base in I Corps.

## MEDAL OF HONOR

**Leo K Thorsness – April 19, 1967**

F-105 pilot Leo K Thorsness risked his life to assist in the rescue of downed aviators over North Vietnam.

On April 19, 1967, Major Thorsness and his Electronic Warfare Officer, Captain Harold E Johnson, flying an F-105F Thunderchief, led the four F-105s on a Wild Weasel SAM suppression mission. Their target was the Xuan Mai army training compound, near heavily defended Hanoi. Two of the jets flew north while Thorsness and his wingman manoeuvred south, forcing the defending gunners to divide their attention. Thorsness located two SAM sites and fired a Shrike missile at the first one, whose radar went off the air. He destroyed the second with cluster bombs.

Soon afterwards 'Kingfish 02', crewed by Majors Thomas M Madison and Thomas J. Sterling, was hit by anti-aircraft fire and both crewmen had to eject. Unknown to Thorsness, 'Kingfish 03' and 'Kingfish 04' had been attacked by MiG-17s. The afterburner of one of the F-105s wouldn't light and the pair had to disengage and return to base, leaving Thorsness ('Kingfish 01') alone.

As he circled the parachutes, relaying the position to the airborne search and rescue command HC-130, Johnson spotted a MiG-17 off their right wing. Although the Thunderchief was not designed for air-to-air combat, Thorsness attacked the MiG and destroyed it with 20-mm cannon fire, just as a second MiG closed on his tail. Low on fuel, Thorsness outran his pursuers and left the battle area to rendezvous with a KC-135 tanker over Laos.

On April 30, 1967, on his 93rd mission (seven shy of completing his tour), Thorsness was shot down by a MiG-21 over North Vietnam and spent six years in captivity as a prisoner of war. Thorsness' Medal of Honor was awarded by Congress during his captivity, but not announced until his release in 1973 to prevent the Vietnamese from using it against him. Captain Johnson received the Air Force Cross for the same mission.

A battle damaged Skyraider comes to rest on the runway at Da Nang as an HH-43 hovers nearby ready to deploy its fire fighting equipment.

▲ The 604th Air Commando Squadron operated the Cessna A-37B Dragonfly from Bien Hoa until September 1970

►A Skyraider from the 1st Air Commando Squadron. The unit was based at Nakhon Phanom and used the call sign Hobo

The Sea Stallion replaced the ageing CH-37 in the helicopter recovery role and was capable of lifting any US Marine helicopter in Vietnam. Between January and May, Detachment A had retrieved 103 helicopters, including 72 UH-34s, enough to equip three medium transport squadrons.

The first of the new Cessna O-2B Psy-Ops aircraft arrived at Nha Trang on May 20. These were equipped with three 600-watt amplifiers and a hand-operated leaflet dispenser. The O-2A FAC models began to arrive at Binh Thuy two weeks later, to act as a stopgap replacement for the venerable O-1 Bird Dog, until the North American OV-10A arrived on the scene. The O-2 was a twin-boom, two-seat observation aircraft with engines mounted fore and aft of the cabin.

### Sandy Skyraiders

By mid-1967 the aircraft with the highest overall loss rate in Southeast Asia was the Douglas A-1E Skyraider. The losses per 1,000 sorties ranged from 1.0 in South Vietnam, to 2.3 over Laos and up to 6.2 for missions over North Vietnam.

The report of a pilot downed usually led to the immediate despatch of an H-3 SAR helicopter, escorted by two Sandy A-1Es. Although they were ideal escorts for the slow-moving helicopter, the Skyraiders were extremely vulnerable to the sophisticated enemy anti-aircraft defences. Of the 25 A-1s shot down over the North between June 1966 and June 1968, seven were lost on rescue missions.

During the month of May, 16 MiG-17s and five MiG-21s were shot down over North Vietnam – including three claimed by *Wolfpack* commander Colonel Robin Olds.

The first of the new F-4D Phantoms joined the 555th TFS at Ubon in Thailand on May 28. Although they could launch the AGM-62 TV-guided Walleye missile against ground targets, they were still not equipped with guns for aerial combat but fortunately the SUU-16A gun pod with its 20mm M61 cannon now began to arrive in the theatre. In July, another 20 F-4Ds arrived at Ubon to replace the F-104s of the 435th TFS. On June 9, one of the unit's F-104s had become the first in the world to acquire 3,000 hours of flying time after a mission over North Vietnam.

## MEDAL OF HONOR

**Gerald O Young – November 8, 1967**

Gerald O Young, a Captain in the 37th Air Rescue and Recovery Squadron was awarded the Medal of Honor for his actions flying a HH-3E helicopter whilst attempting to rescue a Special Forces team in Laos.
When a small American-Vietnamese Road-Watch team was ambushed by the NVA near the Ho Chi Minh Trail just across the border in Laos on November 8, 1967 their request for help was answered by a VNAF H-34 helicopter and an Army UH-1B Huey gunship.

Both helicopters were shot down but the NVA did not move in to kill the surviving team members, nor the seven men from the downed helicopters; they waited instead for more rescue forces to arrive.

Around midnight, under the light of flares dropped by a C-130 control ship, the first of a pair of HH-3E Jolly Green Giants swooped down to pick up the team. As three survivors scrambled aboard, the helicopter was raked with AK-47 fire from point blank range by enemy troops who had crept close to the position. Leaking fuel and oil, the 'Jolly 29' struggled aloft and headed for the Marine base at Khe Sanh.

The commander recommended to Captain Young, the pilot of 'Jolly 26', that further rescue attempts be abandoned, because it was not possible to suppress the concentrated fire from the enemy automatic weapons. However, at least two wounded Americans were still on the ground and with full knowledge of the danger involved (and the fact that supporting helicopter gunships were low on fuel and ordnance), Young decided to go in.

The helicopter was repeatedly hit by enemy fire, including a grenade that sent HH-3E rolling down into a steep ravine, where it burst into flames. Captain Young, hanging upside down in his harness, finally escaped through the broken windshield, his clothing on fire. He rolled down the slope to extinguish the flames, which had inflicted second and third degree burns to his body. He then used his bare hands to smother the flames enveloping an unconscious survivor nearby, before dragging him into hiding. Despite his efforts Young was the only survivor of the crash. Remarkably, he evaded capture for 17 hours until being rescued later that day.

**The Marine Heavy Lift Squadron HMH-463 arrive at Marble Mountain with its 22 Sikorsky CH-53A Sea Stallion helicopters**

**Lt Patton from Navy Attack Squadron VA-176 on the USS Saratoga admires the MiG-21 Kill marking painted on the fuselage of his A-1H Skyraider. He was the second Skyraider pilot to shoot down a MiG**

## Misty Sabres

Operation *Commando Sabre*, the use of two seat F-100F Super Sabres as high-speed Forward Air Control (FAC) aircraft was initiated on June 28. Using the callsign Misty, the F-100s operated in high threat areas where normal FAC aircraft could not survive. One month later the first two-seat Cessna A-37A Dragonfly light strike aircraft arrived in Vietnam. The 25 aircraft of the *Combat Dragon* deployment were flown by the 604th Air Commando Squadron and joined the 3rd TFW at Bien Hoa.

July 1967 saw a number of tragedies occur, starting when two B-52s collided in flight south-east of Saigon on July 7. Among the casualties was Major General William J Crumm, commander of the Strategic Air Command's 3rd Air Division at Anderson AFB, Guam.

Da Nang Air Base suffered an enemy rocket attack on the July 16, which killed eight men and wounded 138 others. Heavy damage was inflicted on the bomb storage area and eleven aircraft were destroyed and 31 damaged.

Just over a week later, on July 25, the aircraft carrier USS *Forrestal* arrived at Yankee Station on her first combat deployment. On board was Air Wing 17, comprising two F-4B and two A-4E squadrons, one RA-5C Vigilante squadron, plus detachments of KA-3B Skywarriors and E-2A Hawkeyes.

A revised *Rolling Thunder* target list had also just been approved, permitting attacks on 16 additional fixed targets and 23 road, rail and waterway segments inside the restricted Hanoi-Haiphong area.

The carrier began operations immediately and flew 150 sorties over the next four days, without loss. However, just before 11.00hrs on the July 29, as a second launch was being prepared, a Zuni rocket was accidentally fired from an F-4 at the aft end of the flight deck. The rocket struck an A-4's fuel tank, which exploded, spreading flames over half of the flight deck. Some 134 men lost their lives, 21 aircraft were destroyed and 43 others damaged. The *Forrestal* left the area and arrived back at Norfolk, Virginia for repairs on September 14.

## Paul Doumer Bridge

The *Rolling Thunder* target list still only contained 16 of the 274 most lucrative

**Just four days after the USS *Forrestal* arrived on Yankee Station, a Zuni rocket was accidentally fired from an F-4 at the aft end of the flight deck. The rocket struck an A-4's fuel tank, which exploded spreading flames over half of the flight deck**

targets in the Hanoi/Haiphong areas. However, it did include the 5,532ft-long 19-span Paul Doumer Bridge across the Red River on the outskirts of Hanoi. It carried two highways and a rail track and all the supplies coming into Hanoi passed over it.

On August 11, a flight of 36 F-105Ds from the 355th and 388th TFWs attacked the bridge with 3,000lb bombs. As Phantoms from the 8th TFW flew MiG-CAP over the strike force and dropped bombs on the anti-aircraft emplacements, Wild Weasel F-105s engaged the SAM sites. Only two of the strike force (both Thunderchiefs) were slightly damaged and as they headed for home, one railway and two highway spans lay in the river.

Seven weeks later, the bridge was in use again but after further raids in October and December, the enemy gave up repairing it and built a pontoon replacement to carry rail traffic five miles away.

With the bridge out of action, the North Vietnamese began to ferry freight across the river by ferry and one dark night in October an A-6 Intruder from the USS *Constellation* was sent to destroy the rail ferry loading slip. Carrying 18,500lb bombs, the Intruder evaded 16 SAM missiles on the way in, dived down to rooftop height, found the ferry slip (docking facility) in the darkness and dropped its bomb load directly on it. Whereas most fighter-bomber aircraft were designed to attack targets that the pilot had to acquire visually, the A-6 possessed a radar system allowing its pilot to attack a target using radar alone.

In August, another MiG deterrent would arrive, in the shape of the EC-121M Rivet Top aircraft, which could detect a MiG taking off and report its position to US aircraft in the area.

## Jolly Green Giants

On September 14, 1967 the first two Sikorsky HH-53B Super Jolly Green Giant helicopters arrived at Vung Tau in South Vietnam. They soon joined Detachment 2, 37th Aerospace Rescue and Recovery Squadron at Udorn and on one occasion a HH-53B lifted a 12,000lb A-1E Skyraider and carried it 56 miles from the central Laotian panhandle to Nakhon Phanom. It was also capable of in-flight refuelling, had excellent range, improved armour protection in vital areas and three GAU-2B/A miniguns, each capable of firing 4,000 rounds per minute.

## MEDAL OF HONOR

**Michael J Estocin – April 26, 1967**

A-4 Skyhawk pilot Lt Commander Michael J Estocin was posthumously awarded the Medal of Honor for his actions over Hanoi on April 20 and 26, 1967 while suppressing SAM sites.

Estocin was one of VFA-192's six *Iron Hand* AGM-45 Shrike pilots aboard the USS *Ticonderoga* in the Gulf of Tonkin. His mission was to target SAM sites, 5-7 minutes ahead of a strike group to try to draw fire from the missile operators.

On April 20, 1967 Estocin led a group of three aircraft in support of a coordinated strike against two thermal power plants in Haiphong, North Vietnam. He provided continuous warnings to the strike group leaders of the SAM threats and personally neutralised three sites. Although his aircraft was severely damaged by an exploding missile, Estocin re-entered the target area and launched his Shrike missile in the face of intense anti-aircraft fire. With less than five minutes of fuel remaining, he left the target area and began in-flight refuelling, which continued for over 100 miles. Three miles from the *Ticonderoga* and without enough fuel for a second approach, he disengaged from the tanker and executed a precise approach to a fiery arrested landing on the carrier's deck.

Six days later, Estocin supported a strike aimed at Haiphong's thermal power station with John B Nichols acting as his escort in an F-8 Crusader. The strike went off without incident, and the two pilots were about to head back to the *Ticonderoga* when Estocin detected an active SAM site. A single missile was launched from the site and exploded near his A-4, knocking it into a barrel roll. Estocin was able to regain control of the burning aircraft and Nichols called for a helicopter rescue.

He flew beside the stricken plane, getting close enough to see Estocin in the cockpit, not moving. As the A-4 lost altitude and entered cloud, Nichols continued to follow it, even as a second SAM exploded nearby. Estocin's jet impacted the ground and Nichols circled the area looking for a parachute. He saw nothing and returned to the *Ticonderoga*.

For his actions Estocin was promoted to captain in absentia and awarded the Medal of Honor

One of the most shocking photographs to come out of the Vietnam War. This C-7 Caribou has been hit by American artillery shells over Ha Phan on August 3, 1967. All three crew on board were killed

An AC-130A Spectre gunship of the 16th Special Operations Squadron at Ubon opens fire with its 20mm Vulcan cannon

## MEDAL OF HONOR

**Lance P Sijan – November 9, 1967**

Weapons System Operator Captain Lance P Sijan was awarded the Medal of Honor posthumously for his actions whilst a prisoner of war.

On the night of November 9, 1967 Captain Sijan and his pilot Lt Col John Armstrong were flying an F-4C with the 366th TFW on a bombing mission over North Vietnam. As they rolled in on their target, their aircraft caught fire when the bomb fuses malfunctioned, causing a premature detonation on their release. Sijan managed to eject from the aircraft, but despite extensive search and rescue efforts it proved impossible to recover him from the jungle.

Sijan had suffered a fractured skull, a mangled right hand, and a compound fracture of the left leg from his rough landing. He was without food, with very little water, and no survival kit; nevertheless, he evaded enemy forces for 46 days. He was finally captured by the North Vietnamese on Christmas Day, 1967. Emaciated and in poor health, he still managed to overpower his guard and escape, but was recaptured several hours later.

He suffered beatings and extensive torture by his captors, but never gave any information other than what the Geneva Convention allowed. Suffering from exhaustion, malnutrition, and disease, he was sent to the notorious Hanoi Hilton – the Hoa Lo Prison in Hanoi – where he contracted pneumonia and died on January 22, 1968. Sijan's remains were repatriated in March 1974 and his family received the Medal of Honor on his behalf on March 4, 1976 from President Gerald R Ford.

◄ As fast as US air power destroyed the roads and bridges along the Ho Chi Minh Trail, the North Vietnamese would repair them.

► The USS *Ranger* arrived on Yankee Station on December 3, with the new Vought A-7A Corsair II on board. They belonged to VA-147, the first operational Corsair squadron and flew their first combat mission a day later. This picture was taken on the USS *Constellation* and shows a Corsair of Navy Attack Squadron VA-97 waiting behind a Corsair from VA-27 about to launch from the bow catapult

## MEDAL OF HONOR

**Merlyn H Dethlefsen – March 10, 1967**

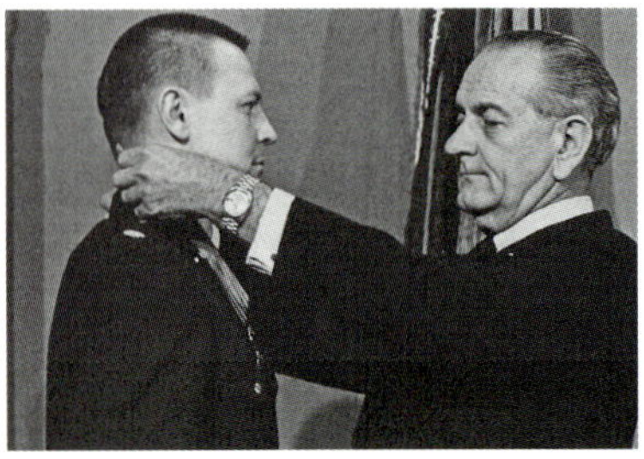

Captain Merlyn H Dethlefsen received the Medal of Honor for repeated close range strikes to silence enemy defensive positions, ignoring overwhelming firepower and damage to his own aircraft.

On March 10, 1967 Dethlefsen and the three other F-105 Thunderchiefs of Lincoln Flight, flew ahead of a strike force of 72 fighter-bombers heading for the Thai Nguyen iron and steel works in North Vietnam. His role was to attack the surface-to-air missile sites and anti-aircraft guns guarding the target but on the first pass his flight leader was shot down and the downed F-105's wingman also had to head home with severe damage. Although Dethlefsen's aircraft too was damaged, he took command of the flight while enemy MiG-21s rose to meet them. He evaded one MiG-21 by flying into heavy anti-aircraft fire, damaging his jet again. Despite this, Dethlefsen and his wingman continued to attack the enemy anti-aircraft sites, destroying two sites before he finally turned for home – 500 miles away.

For his heroism, Dethlefsen was awarded the Medal of Honor by President Lyndon B Johnson on February 1, 1968.

**Col Robert Maloy (left) and Capt William S Paul (right) of the 366th Tactical Fighter Wing after being rescued by an HH-3E Jolly Green Giant from the 37th Aerospace Rescue and Recovery Squadron on October 15, 1967. Enemy fire hit their F-4 Phantom over North Vietnam, but they reached open water before ejecting. Maloy fractured his back, and Para-rescue-man Roger Klenovich (centre, wearing red beret) went into the water to help him** *(USAF Museum)*

**Sensors dropped over the Ho Chi Minh Trail would pick up the sounds and movements of enemy vehicles and personnel, and transmit automatically to orbiting EC-121R Batcats which would relay the information back to Nakhon Phanom**

Six additional HH-53Bs reached Southeast Asia before the HH-53C, the ultimate rescue helicopter, arrived in September 1969.

The HU-16B Albatross flew its last SAR mission in the same month that the HH-53Bs arrived. During five years in Southeast Asia, four HU-16s had been lost, together with nine crewmembers. On the credit side, they had rescued 47 Navy and USAF aircrew. Soon the first HC-130P aircraft would arrive to replace the HC-130Hs in the airborne mission control role. The HC-130P was equipped with internal fuel tanks, pumps and drogues to also enable it to refuel HH-3 and HH-53 helicopters in the air.

### Spectre

Another version of the C-130 was the AC-130 Gunship II, nicknamed the Spectre. Planned as a successor to the AC-47 Spooky and later joined by the AC-119G Shadow and AC-119K Stinger, the first test AC-130 arrived at Nha Trang on September 20. A week later, the Spectre flew its first mission, supporting troops in contact at a fire-support base in South Vietnam.

The aircraft proved so successful in the truck-hunting role that a contract was issued to modify seven other early JC-130As into gunships with four 20mm GE M61 Gatling cannons and four 7.62mm GE MXU-470 miniguns. The aircraft also had a Night Observation Device (NOD) or starlight scope, a primitive infrared sensor and a 20kw searchlight.

During September 1967, the VNAF began to receive a squadron of Fairchild C-119 Flying Boxcar transports. Later they would receive 18 AC-47 gunships as the USAF converted to more modern types and the VNAF would eventually possess two squadrons of AC-119s and one of AC-47s. The Bell UH-1 Huey also began to replace the VNAF's ageing H-34 helicopters.

### Milestones

USAF combat sorties in South Vietnam exceeded the one million mark in September 1967. By October 16, there were 1,500 aircraft deployed to Southeast Asia and three days later the total aircraft losses passed the 1,000 mark.

Back in the USA, opposition to the war had increased and on October 21 some 50,000 anti-war demonstrators marched on the Pentagon.

Meanwhile, the Preparedness Subcommittee of the Senate Armed Services Committee had conducted extensive hearings in August, into the conduct of the air war against North Vietnam. Secretary McNamara, who would resign at the end of the year, defended the Administration's policy of gradual escalation. Top military leaders involved in the Rolling Thunder campaign put forward their arguments for an escalation of the attacks, and their opinions were largely endorsed by the committee.

President Johnson took the hint and approved an attack on North Vietnam's third port at Cam Pha on September 10. However, MiG opposition was increasing rapidly and on the October 24 a strike against Phuc Yen air base was finally approved. The following day a joint Navy and USAF raid destroyed nine MiGs on the ground and rendered the base unusable.

Air strikes continued against every jet-capable airfield in North Vietnam, except Hanoi's international Gia Lam airport. However, many of the MiGs were dispersed to bases in China while repairs were made to their own airfields and losses were made up with replacements.

Earlier in the month President Johnson had asked the JCS what could be done to put more pressure on Hanoi. They proposed a ten-point list of suggestions, including the removal of all restrictions on significant military targets, the mining of North Vietnamese ports and waterways, and the expansion of operations into Laos and Cambodia. The JCS would not have many more chances to try to change the President's strategy into one that might have succeeded. However, their ten recommendations were rejected and five months later, in March 1968, US de-escalation began.

## *Igloo White*

In the meantime, US air operations continued over Laos in an attempt to stem the flow of men and supplies down the Ho Chi Minh Trail to South Vietnam. A rudimentary, air supported, electronic anti-infiltration system came into being towards the end of 1967, designed to detect enemy movements on the Trail. The programme was given a succession of nicknames including *Muscle Shoals*, *Mud River* and *Dump Truck*, but *Igloo White* was the best known and used the longest.

Strings of seismic and acoustic sensors were air-dropped in designated jungle areas, where they would pick up the sounds and movements of enemy vehicles and personnel, and transmit automatically to orbiting aircraft, such as EC-121R Batcats and later Beechcraft QU-22 Bonanzas. The aircraft would relay the information back to the Infiltration Surveillance Centre, knows as the Dutch Mill because of the unique shape of its antenna, at Nakhon Phanom.

The Centre's computers would interpret the signals and produce information on the volume of traffic, convoy speed and hours of operation. Interdiction aircraft would then be sent to that area to fix and destroy the supply trucks or infiltrating troops.

In November, the first modified Lockheed OP-2E Neptunes from Navy Observation Squadron VO-67 arrived at Nakhon Phanom. They wore dark jungle green camouflage and were to be used to drop the sensors along the Ho Chi Minh Trail. Unfortunately, the slow-moving Neptunes were easy meat for the enemy anti-aircraft gunners and before long three had been lost. The unit was disestablished in July 1968 and its role was taken over by the F-4s of the 25th TFS.

On the ground, the big battles of 1967 had brought the number of US troops killed so far to over 16,000 and the latter months of the year saw gruelling marches into the western depths of Kontum Province where the North Vietnamese Army (NVA) were firmly entrenched in bunker complexes. In November, an enemy mortar attack on Dak To airfield set off the ammunition dump and destroyed two C-130 cargo aircraft.

On November 18, the fight for Hill 875 began and became the climax of the Battle of Dak To and the 1967 campaign for the Highlands. The fanatical 174th NVA Regiment held the hill and decimated the attacking Americans. A misplaced bomb from a USAF airstrike also killed or badly wounded 50 paratroopers and the 335th Aviation Company had six of its helicopters shot down as they brought in reinforcements. On November 21, the USAF dropped seven and a half tons of napalm on the NVA defenders and continued their airstrikes throughout the whole of the following day. US paratroopers reached the summit of the hill on the morning of October 23, but the battle had involved 2,096 tactical air sorties, 257 B-52 bombing strikes and the Chinooks of the 179th Aviation Company recovered the carcasses of over 40 downed helicopters.

**In November the first modified Lockheed OP-2E Neptunes from Navy Observation Squadron VO-67 arrived at Nakhon Phanom RTAFB. They wore dark jungle green camouflage and were to be used to drop the sensors along the Ho Chi Minh Trail. Unfortunately, the slow-moving Neptunes were easy meat for the enemy anti-aircraft gunners and before long three had been lost**

## Corsair II

The US aircraft carrier *Ranger* arrived on Yankee Station on December 3, bringing with it the new Vought A-7A Corsair II on board. The jets belonged to VA-147, the first operational Corsair squadron and flew their first combat mission a day later. By now the monsoon season had begun again in the North and the bad flying conditions caused a reduction in combat sorties, with only the A-6s flying on a regular basis. The enemy defences claimed the first A-7A to ground-fire on December 22 and the surface-to-air missile (SAM) threat renewed as the North Vietnamese began installing optical tracking devices on their SAM guidance systems, severely degrading the effectiveness of the ECM pods.

During 1966 the USAF lost 421 aircraft in Southeast Asia, including 113 F-105s and 95 F-4s. The enemy had launched 16 attacks on air bases throughout the year and destroyed or damaged 81 aircraft on the ground. The USAF had flown 878,771 combat sorties (an increase of 69% over 1966) and 681,000 tons of munitions had been expended – up 87% on the previous year.

By now 485,000 US military personnel were in Vietnam and the war appeared to be going well – or so they thought. ❖

## MEDAL OF HONOR

**Stephen Pless – August 19, 1967**

Helicopter gunship pilot Captain Stephen Pless became the first and only Marine aviator to be awarded the Medal of Honor when he rescued four wounded men who were about to be killed by the enemy.

On August 19, 1967, Captain Pless was piloting a UH-1E gunship from Marine Observation Squadron VMO-6 on an escort mission in the vicinity of Quang Ngai, when he monitored an emergency call for assistance from four Army helicopter crewmen stranded on a nearby beach. They were being overrun by a force of between 40 and 50 Viet Cong and by the time that Pless arrived on the scene the fighting had developed to close quarters and the Viet Cong were bayoneting and beating the men on the ground.

Pless immediately opened fire with machine guns and rockets and drove the enemy away from the Americans. His rocket and machine gun firing runs were made at such low-level that he flew through the debris created by explosions from his rockets.

Despite intense enemy fire, Pless landed his helicopter on the beach. The gunner, (Leroy N Poulson) jumped on to the beach and assisted the only American capable of walking back to the helicopter. The crew chief continued firing at the Viet Cong who were moving towards the rear of the helicopter. Then he, also, jumped out to help carry the remaining three men. By now three Viet Cong fighters were killed less than 10ft away from the helicopter just before Pless lifted the overloaded Huey into the air.The helicopter was so heavy it settled into the water four times before finally taking to the air.

Pless was awarded the Medal of Honor in January 1969, and the other members of his crew received the Navy Cross. Sadly, having survived being shot down twice and hit by enemy fire on 97 occasions, Pless was killed in a motorcycle accident in Florida just six months later.

# THE DEADLIEST YEAR

**The highest death toll of US military personnel was recorded in 1968. The decisive victory in the Tet Offensive was also a turning point in the war – but not for the right reasons**

**Used extensively over South Vietnam and Laos, the USAF OV-10 FACs were particularly useful over the Ho Chi Minh Trail, where their laser designators could pinpoint targets at night, for jets carrying laser-guided bombs**

In late January 1968, North Korean gunboats seized the USS *Pueblo* in the Sea of Japan off Korea. The following day President Johnson ordered the mobilisation of eleven Air National Guard (ANG) F-100 Super Sabre squadrons – two of which were sent to South Korea and four others were deployed to South Vietnam.

The battle of Khe Sanh also began on January 21, 1968 when the North Vietnamese unleashed a heavy mortar, artillery and rocket attack on the now-famous US Marine Corps (USMC) base and its outlying defences.

Khe Sanh was located on a plateau in the north-western corner of I Corps and commanded the approaches to Dong Ha and Quang Tri City and the coastal corridor leading to Hue. By capturing this important strategic outpost, the North Vietnamese Army (NVA) would have an almost unobstructed invasion route in the northernmost provinces, from where they could outflank American positions south of the demilitarised zone (DMZ).

NVA General Giap also hoped to emulate his great Viet Minh victory over the French at Dien Bien Phu 14 years earlier. This time though, things would be different; the French had been short of tactical air support but the Americans had plenty standing by.

Operation *Niagara* began with an average of 300 tactical sorties each day, including, at the height of the battle, the arrival of three B-52s every 90 minutes.

Resupply was not easy though, as the lumbering C-123 and C-130 transport aircraft were easy targets for the enemy gunners. One C-123 was shot down, killing all 48 personnel on board and a Marine KC-130 carrying fuel was hit and crashed, with only two survivors. Over a two and a half month period, more than 24,000 tactical and 2,700 B-52 sorties dropped 110,000 tons of ordnance in defence of the base.

## Sneak attack

On January 30, nine days after the siege of Khe Sanh began, the Tet celebration of the lunar New Year started. It was South Vietnam's biggest annual holiday and for over a week all business and Government would stop. President Thieu left Saigon to spend the holiday with relatives in the Mekong Delta and almost half of the 732,000 strong armed forces went on leave.

**The Bell AH-1G Cobra was an improvement over the Huey gunships in that it was much narrower and presented a smaller target to the enemy on the ground. This Cobra flown by Randy Zahn is fitted with seven and 19-shot rocket pods** *(Randy Zahn via Phil Chinnery)*

**The first deployment of the F-111A was not a success and three aircraft were lost within a month**

A 36-hour ceasefire was called but just as it was a supposed to come into effect, all hell broke loose. Viet Cong and North Vietnamese forces attacked nearly every important city, provincial capital and military installation in South Vietnam.

Even the American Embassy in Saigon was attacked by a suicide squad of Viet Cong sappers (combat engineers). They breached the walls but failed to gain entry to the Chancery.

Nearly 700 enemy troops attacked Tan Son Nhut Air Base in two battalions of Viet Cong and NVA troops attacked Bien Hoa Air Base. Unfortunately for the troops attacking Bien Hoa, the base was playing host to the new Bell AH-1G Cobra gunship New Equipment Training Team (NETT), which had arrived with the first six Cobras four months before.

The new gunship was a vast improvement over the armed UH-1s; with a frontal area only three feet wide and a crew of two seated in tandem, it presented a much smaller target to enemy gunners. It was armed with a revolving turret under the nose, equipped with a minigun and 40mm grenade launcher and could carry a variety of gun and rocket pods on short wing stubs behind the cockpit. The 334th Assault Helicopter Company had begun to convert to the new gunship and when the enemy attack began, they took to the air with a vengeance. The communist losses were tremendous with 139 killed at the base and a further 1,164 in the surrounding area.

American and South Vietnamese forces regained control quite rapidly, although the extent of the Tet Offensive had clearly caught them by surprise. The communists captured part of the city of Hue, including the Citadel, and held on for a month, during which time they slaughtered over 3,000 innocent civilians. By the time they had been driven from the city, much of the ancient capital of Vietnam had been destroyed.

In just two weeks the communists lost 32,000 men and a further 5,800 were captured. Conversely 1,001 US troops were lost and South Vietnamese and Allied losses were put at 2,082. The greatest effect of the Tet Offensive was felt, however, not in Vietnam, but in Washington.

**This F-4 came in for a wheels-up landing at Cam Ranh Bay in June 1968. The foam-covered runway limited the damage to the aircraft**

## State of shock

The siege of Khe Sanh and the Tet Offensive sent the Washington Administration into a state of shock. Hanoi had taken a big gamble and had lost on the battlefield, but they had won a psychological victory in the USA. The American public began to voice its dissatisfaction with the war.

The opinions of the media and anti-war protesters not withstanding, the USA was now in an excellent position to win the war in South Vietnam. The Viet Cong and North Vietnamese forces in the South had suffered huge losses during the Tet Offensive and it would take time to restore their pre-Tet manpower and supply levels. Now was the time to abolish the prohibited zones around Hanoi and Haiphong and along the border with China. The major ports and harbours could be mined to cut off outside support to the North and a major air campaign without restrictions could destroy the war-making capability of North Vietnam and punish it sufficiently to halt its insurgency in the South.

The civilian leaders in Washington, however, saw things differently. The biased and often misleading media coverage of the siege at Khe Sanh and the Tet Offensive had increased public pressure on the Johnson Administration to end the war. To devote the number of troops required to win the war would have meant mobilisation and in an election year, that was not going to happen.

## MEDAL OF HONOR

**Patrick Brady – January 6, 1968**

Huey medevac pilot Capt Patrick Brady was awarded the Medal of Honor for using three helicopters to rescue 51 wounded men in 24 hours.

He volunteered to rescue wounded men from a site in enemy-held territory, which was reported to be heavily defended. To reach the site he descended through heavy fog and smoke and hovered slowly along a valley trail, turning his helicopter sideways to blow away the fog with the backwash from his rotor blades. Despite the close-range enemy fire, Brady found the dangerously small site, where he successfully landed and evacuated two badly wounded South Vietnamese soldiers. He was then called to another area completely covered by dense fog where American casualties lay only 50m from the enemy. Two aircraft had previously been shot down and others had made unsuccessful attempts to reach this site earlier in the day. With unmatched skill and extraordinary courage, Brady made four flights to this embattled landing zone and successfully rescued all the wounded. On his third mission of the day, Brady once again landed at a site surrounded by the enemy – twice. Although his aircraft had been badly damaged and his controls partially shot away during his initial entry into this area, he returned minutes later and rescued the remaining injured.

Having obtained a replacement aircraft, Brady was requested to land in an enemy minefield where a platoon of American soldiers was trapped. A mine detonated near his helicopter, wounding two crewmembers and damaging his helicopter. In spite of this, he managed to fly six severely injured patients to medical aid.

During his two tours in Vietnam Brady flew over 2,000 combat missions and evacuated more than 5,000 wounded.

A Navy A-7E Corsair from VA-147 flying off the USS *Constellation* joins an A-6A Intruder from VA-165 on a bombing mission over North Vietnam

## MEDAL OF HONOR

**Frederick E Ferguson – January 31, 1968**

Frederick E Ferguson risked his life by flying his helicopter into heavy enemy fire at Hue to evacuate several wounded passengers and the aircrew of a downed helicopter. Although his helicopter was severely damaged by mortar fragments during the loading of the wounded, Ferguson disregarded the damage and, taking off through the continuing hail of mortar fire, flew his crippled aircraft to friendly territory - returning his wounded passengers to safety.

The early AC-47 gunships were later passed on to the Vietnamese Air Force as well as the Royal Lao Air Force. This crew is part of the RLAF 1st Ghost Squadron

The President and his advisers yet again turned a deaf ear to the advice of the Joint Chiefs of Staff (JCS) and on March 31, President Johnson announced that, in an attempt to persuade the North Vietnamese to begin peace negotiations, all bombing north of the 20th Parallel was to cease forthwith.

Towards the end of his speech, Johnson also announced that he would neither seek, nor accept, the nomination of his party for another term as President.

Shortly after the *Rolling Thunder* operations north of the 20th Parallel were halted, the US media denounced a naval air raid on transportation facilities near Thanh Hóa , an important communications and traffic centre just south of the 20-degree line. In order to appease the media the demarcation line was lowered still further to the 19th Parallel.

## Turning point

President Johnson's March 31 speech marked a major turning point in the war. American policy was now committed to a negotiated, as opposed to a military settlement of the war and this new policy began with major concessions to the enemy.

The North Vietnamese response to the limiting of the bombing campaign to the relatively target-free area just north of the DMZ was to increase the amount of supplies flowing south; improve its anti-aircraft defences and start to infiltrate 75,000 replacement troops down the Trail.

Two weeks before President Johnson's speech on the war, on March 15, six General Dynamics F-111A swing-wing fighter-bombers arrived at Takhli air base. The new aircraft were Detachment 1 of the 428th TFS from the 474th TFW at Nellis AFB in Nevada and their deployment went by the name of *Combat Lancer*.

The F-111 was equipped with terrain-following radar, which would enable it to deliver a full load of 24 500lb bombs on any target, in any weather, by flying undetected under enemy radar. Sadly, three of the *Combat Lancer* aircraft were lost within a month and the detachment returned home by the end of the year. At least two of the losses were caused by tailplane failure due to fatigue at a welding joint, and this, and other problems, prevented the return of the F-111 to Southeast Asia until September 1972.

## Operation *Delaware*

US forces returned to the A Shau Valley on April 19 during Operation *Delaware*. Since March 1966, the North Vietnamese had used the area as a supply and staging base for attacks into I and II Corps and had constructed elaborate defences and anti-aircraft sites around the valley.

Now the US Army's 1st Cavalry and 101st Airborne Divisions carried out a major airmobile assault in the northern end of the valley while the 1st Army of the Republic of Vietnam (ARVN) Division approached from the east.

The weather was unbelievably bad and the anti-aircraft fire was so intense that by the time the operation ended on May 17, the 1st Cavalry Division alone had lost 21 helicopters. However, the operation was

By the end of July 1968 some 382 US pilots and 289 aircrew had been killed and 702 were listed as missing. Many of the missing were now guests of the North Vietnamese in prisoner of war camps, where beatings and torture were commonplace

## MEDAL OF HONOR

**Gary Wetzel – January 8, 1968**

Despite his left arm almost being severed and repeatedly losing consciousness from loss of blood after the helicopter he was on was shot down, Private Gary Wetzel fought against enemy gun emplacement and assisted in the rescue of a fallen officer.

North Vietnamese troops examine the wreckage of a US jet brought down by ground fire in South Vietnam

North Vietnamese troops inspect the wreckage of a Navy jet, possibly an F-8 Crusader, with the name Lt J G Greene on the side

a success – at least in the short term – as the enemy retreated over the border, abandoning a mountain of supplies. More than 900 communists were killed against 100 Allied dead and one million rounds of ammunition and 3,000 individual weapons were captured.

## Abandoning Khe Sanh

US forces had started to replenish and relieve the besieged base at Khe Sanh with Operation *Pegasus* on April 1. The weather had improved by then but the enemy had already had enough and withdrawn.

As it happened, the combat base had been dismantled and abandoned by June 23. Despite the vast expenditure of munitions and supplies in support of the besieged Marines in February and March, the base had outlived its usefulness.

The first of the new twin-turboprop OV-10A Bronco aircraft arrived at Da Nang on July 6. They were used by the USMC's VMO-2 (and later VMO-6) at Marble Mountain in conjunction with the AH-1G Cobra to take over the role of the UH-1E Huey armed helicopters.

The Bronco could be armed with 3,600lbs of guns, bombs and rockets and by the end of July 1968 the USAF had also received their first OV-10s to be used in the Forward Air Controller role. The USAF OV-10 FACs were deployed extensively over South Vietnam and Laos and were particularly useful over the Ho Chi Minh Trail, where their laser designators could pinpoint targets at night, for jets carrying laser-guided bombs.

By 1968, the helicopter observation and reconnaissance role had been taken over by the Hughes OH-6A Cayuse. The Loach, as it became known, replaced the old Bell OH-13 Sioux and Hiller OH-23 Raven, which had suffered losses of 170 and 95 respectively by the war's end, and saw extensive action with the air cavalry troops. Loaches usually worked in a Pink Team formation with a Bell AH-1G Cobra gunship. Flying as armed aero scouts, the Loaches were frequently the first to engage the enemy, a fact reflected in their total war losses of 955, with 658 of those in combat.

On September 7, the 8th TFW at Ubon recorded its 50,000th Southeast Asia combat sortie with a bombing mission over the southern panhandle of North Vietnam. During the same month, *Go Get 'Em*, an F-4D of the 13th TFS at Udorn flew 80 combat sorties over the North, breaking all existing records for the number of sorties flown in a one month period by a Phantom.

## Neptune gunships

The F-102A interceptor detachment at Bien Hoa returned home to Clark AFB on September 25 to ease the strain on the interceptor squadron at Clark, which was also responsible for deployments to Thailand and Korea.

As they departed, another detachment arrived in the shape of four Lockheed AP-2H Neptune gunships. These modified SP-2Hs were a part of the Trails and Road Interdiction, Multisensor (TRIM) programme and were assigned to the Navy's Heavy Attack Squadron VAH-21 at Cam Ranh Bay.

**The F-4E had many improvements over earlier F-4s most notably its internal 20mm gun. The first F-4Es arrived in Southeast Asia in late 1968** *(USAF Museum)*

## MEDAL OF HONOR

**Joe Jackson – May 12, 1968**

C-123 Provider pilot Lt Col Joe Jackson was awarded the Medal of Honor for rescuing a combat control team that had been left stranded on the runway at Kham Duc Special Forces camp as it was overrun by the Viet Cong.

Nine aircraft were lost during the battle for the Kham Duc. On the afternoon of May 12, a C-130 'reinserted' a three-man combat control team that had been withdrawn earlier in the day. They found no survivors and now they needed to be picked up. Lt Col Joe Jackson had been a fighter pilot for twenty years before being assigned to transport duty. He had flown 107 missions in Korea and had won the DFC. He knew that the enemy gunners would expect him to follow the same flight path as the other cargo aeroplanes, and decided to call upon his fighter-pilot experiences and try a new tactic. At 9,000ft and rapidly approaching the landing area he pointed the nose down in a steep dive. Side slipping for maximum descent, with power back and landing gear and flaps full down, the Provider dropped like a rock. He flared at treetop height and landed on the debris-strewn runway, including a burning helicopter blocking the way a mere 600m from the touchdown point. Jackson knew that he would have to stop in a hurry, but decided against using reverse thrust. Reversing the propellers would automatically shut off the two jets that would be needed for a minimum-run take-off. He stood on the brakes and skidded to a halt just before reaching the helicopter.

With the three troops safely aboard a 122mm rocket shell hit the ground just 25ft in front of the aircraft. Luckily it didn't explode and Jackson taxied around the shell and rammed the throttles to the firewall. Within seconds they were in the air again. The C-123 had not taken a single hit!

They were armed with two forward-firing minigun pods, two 500lb bombs and two incendiary bombs mounted under the wings. They also carried a twin 20mm cannon in the tail and were later fitted with a 40mm grenade launcher in the bomb bay.

To carry out their night interdiction role, they were equipped with a Forward Looking Infrared (FLIR) and Low Light Television (LLTV) sensor. A Side-Looking Airborne Radar was mounted on both sides of the fuselage and the tail-gunner used a Night Observation Scope in place of the standard reflector gunsight. The anti-submarine warfare radome had been replaced with an AN/APQ-92 search radar and additional equipment including a Real Time IR sensor, an airborne Moving Target Indicator, DIANE (Digital Integrated Attack and Navigation Equipment) and a Black Crow truck ignition sensor.

Between September 1968 and June 1969, the four SP-2H aircraft flew over 200 missions, mostly in the Parrot's Beak area of the Mekong Delta, but also in Cambodia and Laos against the Ho Chi Minh Trail. All four returned safely to the United States.

The last of 18 MiG kills credited to a Vought F-8 Crusader took place on September 19 when two F-8Cs from VF-111 on the carrier *Intrepid* spotted a pair of MiG-21 *Fishbeds* and climbed to intercept them. Lt Anthony Nargi manoeuvred behind one of the MiGs and fired a Sidewinder missile which blew the entire tail off the enemy fighter as the pilot ejected.

A 19th MiG kill was claimed by a Crusader pilot from the *Hancock* in May 1972, but as the enemy pilot ejected before the F-8 got within firing range, the kill was not approved.

## Change of command

On November 1, 1968, following the advice of his negotiating team in Paris, President Johnson ordered a halt to all bombing of North Vietnam. His negotiators naively believed that they had reached an understanding with the North Vietnamese; that substantive talks would begin as soon as the bombing stopped. They were wrong. The communists began to repair the bridges and roads below the 19th Parallel, strengthen their anti-aircraft defences and improve their airfields. Truck movements of supplies to their troops in the South increased four-fold. However, the *Rolling Thunder* campaign was now finished and although the ground war in the South and the air war over Laos would continue, American bombers would not return to the North again until 1972. Four days later, on November 5, Republican Richard M Nixon

## MEDAL OF HONOR

**Clyde Lassen – June 19, 1968**

Navy pilot Lt Clyde Lassen was awarded the Medal of Honor for flying a UH-2 Seasprite to rescue two downed aviators in North Vietnamese territory.

After ejecting from an F-4J Phantom II hit by a SAM, Lt Cdr John Holtzclaw and radar intercept officer Lt Cdr John Burns, were fighting their way up the slope of a ridge through dense vegetation. Burns was suffering as he had broken his leg during the ejection. It took almost two hours for Lassen to fly to the crash site and home in on the Americans' survival radios. The two men fired a flare and with the aid of the flare's illumination, Lt Lassen brought the UH-2 to a hover between two trees, 50ft above the ground. As they began to lower their hoist, the flare went out, plunging the area into darkness. Lassen added power and was just starting a climb when he hit a tree. Expertly righting his aircraft, Lassen remained in the area, determined to make another rescue attempt.

After another unsuccessful, illuminated rescue attempt, and with his fuel dangerously low and his aircraft significantly damaged, Lassen commenced another approach in the face of the continuing enemy fire. When flare illumination was again lost, and fully aware of the dangers in clearly revealing his position to the enemy, he turned on his landing lights and completed the landing.

For two minutes Lassen held his aircraft in the hover, while his gunners blasted away at the tree line with their machine guns to enable the survivors to make their way to the helicopter. Lt Lassen became the first naval aviator and fifth Navy man to be awarded the Medal of Honor for bravery in Vietnam.

**Sikorsky HH-3E 66-13290, a Jolly Green Giant rescue helicopter of the 37th Air Rescue Squadron at Da Nang in 1968** *(US Navy)*

defeated Democrat Hubert H Humphrey and became the new President of the United States.

### 'Vietnamisation'

As 1968 came to an end the new President and his team prepared to move in to the White House. President Nixon had come to power with a promise to reduce the US commitment in Vietnam and bring America's sons home. The policy was now one of 'Vietnamisation', in which the forces of South Vietnam would be supplied with arms and logistical support to enable them to face up to the North Vietnamese, while the American combat troops withdrew.

Nixon was a strong President and despite the civil unrest and public discontent with the war, he was not about to abandon South Vietnam. He would not restart the *Rolling Thunder* campaign, but during his term of office he would authorise cross-border operations into the enemy sanctuaries in Laos and Cambodia, approve secret bombing raids into Cambodia and when all efforts at finding peace had failed, he would order the mining of the North Vietnamese ports and send the B-52s against Hanoi.

While the new policy was being formulated, the air war over South Vietnam and Laos continued. The fighters and bombers which had been so misused in the *Rolling Thunder* campaign were now available for use against enemy infiltration routes through Laos and Cambodia.

An extensive interdiction campaign called Commando Hunt was begun in Laos on November 15. The campaign was concentrated in the *Barrel Roll* and *Steel Tiger* areas and its objectives were to destroy as much as possible of the supplies being moved down the Trail, to tie down enemy manpower and to test further the effectiveness of the sensor system. The campaign drastically increased the number of sorties flown in Southeast Asia from 4,764 tactical and 273 B-52 sorties in October, to 12,821 and 661 in November.

It is an unfortunate fact that despite the best efforts of the US Air Force, Navy and Marines, the flow of men and material down the Ho Chi Minh Trail actually increased, rather than decreased, every year. To the pilots flying the missions it must have been like trying to beat a snake to death starting at the tail. They were risking their lives hunting for individual trucks coming down the jungle trails, usually in the dark, whereas it would have been a far more effective use of airpower to have sent strikes against the supply bases and ammunition dumps near the ports in North Vietnam, from where the trucks began their journey.

The first AC-119Gs of the *Combat Hornet* deployment arrived at Nha Trang on 22 December and were given the callsign Shadow. They belonged to the 71st Special Operations Squadron

## MEDAL OF HONOR

**James P Fleming – November 26, 1968**

UH-1F Capt James P Fleming was awarded the Medal of Honor for rescuing a Special Forces team surrounded by the enemy near the Cambodian border. A forward air controller and Fleming's flight of five UH-1s were nearby, but all were low on fuel. Hovering just above the jungle treetops, Fleming inspected the only clearing near enough for the troops to reach and found it impossible to land there. He instead flew over the river and hovered just above the water, with his landing skids against the bank, hoping that the special forces troops would be able to run the few yards to his helicopter safely. After waiting for several minutes under heavy fire, the reconnaissance team radioed that they couldn't survive a dash to the helicopter. Fleming lifted his UH-1 out of range of the hostile fire.

The FAC directed the team to detonate their mines as Fleming made a last attempt to rescue them. As the mines exploded, he again lowered his helicopter to the river bank, balancing against it, giving the troops an open cargo door through which to leap to safety. As the enemy soldiers concentrated their fire on the UH-1, the Green Berets dashed for the chopper, firing as they ran and killing three Viet Cong barely 10ft from the aircraft.

## New air assets

New types of aircraft making an appearance over the Trail during November included the RA-3B Skywarrior, the NC-123K Provider, the gun-equipped F-4E Phantom II and the Fairchild AC-119 Gunship III.

The RA-3Bs were from the Navy's Heavy Photographic Squadron VAP-61 and were equipped with infrared sensors so they could roam the trails at night, looking for truck traffic. Flying below 500ft, the RA-3Bs sensors could detect hot spots, indicating traffic on the Trail and then orbiting A-4 Skyhawks would be called in to attack the targets.

The NC-123Ks were equipped with Forward Looking Radar in a 5ft-long nose housing and FLIR, LLTV and a laser illuminator/rangefinder mounted in a sensor turret just aft of the new radome. They were also fitted with weapons release computers and armed with 36 Cluster Bomb Units (CBUs) mounted in dispenser chutes in the aft cargo compartment.

The gun-equipped Phantoms arrived in Southeast Asia on November 17, when 20 F-4Es flew into Korat to join the 469th TFS. The aircraft retained the ability to carry Sparrow/Sidewinder missiles but also had a 640 round 20mm Vulcan cannon in its nose. The pilots would be unable to test the new gun in a dogfight though. With the bombing halt over the North in effect, it would be three more years before another MiG would be downed.

One weapon that could be tested as soon as it arrived was the Fairchild AC-119 Gunship III. The AC-130 was supposed to take over the role of the AC-47, but production delays led to the AC-119 arriving first. Like the AC-47 the AC-119 was built with the Troops In Contact (TIC) support mission in mind and it was armed with four 7.62mm *Minigun* pods. The first AC-119s of the *Combat Hornet* deployment at Nha Trang entered service on December 22 and were given the callsign Shadow.

## Heavy losses

By the end of 1968, the USAF in Southeast Asia had lost another 392 aircraft; 88 to operational causes, 257 to ground fire, 35 were destroyed in attacks on air bases and a dozen were lost to MiGs and SAMs. The latter figure was down from the 40 lost in 1967 and reflected the decrease in air activity over North Vietnam.

During the year 16,511 US military personnel had been killed, the highest number for any year of the war.

Another indication of the intensity of the fighting on the ground is the total of the US Army fixed-wing and helicopter losses for the year. These were up to 1,008; one third more than in 1967. Over 42,000 Medevac helicopter sorties were flown during the year and 67,000 people were rescued or evacuated.

By the end of July 1968, the USAF, Navy and Marines had dropped around 2,500,000 tons of bombs on North Vietnam; 877 fixed wing aircraft and nine helicopters had been lost over North Vietnam in the process.

Over both North and South Vietnam, 382 pilots and 289 aircrew had been killed and 702 were listed as missing. Many of the missing were now guests of the North Vietnamese in prisoner of war camps, where beatings and torture were commonplace.

Phantoms from the 13th and 555th Tactical Fighter Squadrons of the 432nd Tactical Reconnaissance Wing heading North. The two squadrons produced three 'Aces' during the war

By 1968, typical USAF combat rescue packages included strike aircraft, aerial refuellers and rescue helicopters *(USAF Museum)*

A USAF C-130 taking off from Khe Sanh in the midst of the attacks in January 1968 *(USAF Museum)*

## MEDAL OF HONOR

**William A Jones III – September 1, 1968**

Lt Col William A Jones III was awarded the Medal of Honor after flying his badly damaged A-1 Skyraider back to base to relay the location of a downed pilot.

In the attempted rescue of a downed pilot, Jones' aircraft was repeatedly hit by heavy and accurate anti-aircraft fire. On one of his low passes, he felt an explosion beneath his aircraft and his cockpit rapidly filled with smoke. With complete disregard of the possibility that his aircraft might still be burning, he unhesitatingly continued his search for the downed pilot. On this pass he sighted the survivor and a multiple-barrel gun position firing at him from near the top of a karst formation.

He made further passes until automatic weapons fire impacted the ejection seat rocket mounted directly behind the headrest, igniting the rocket. He pulled the extraction handle, jettisoning the canopy. The influx of fresh air made the fire burn with greater intensity for a few moments, but since the rocket motor had already burned, the extraction system did not pull him from the aircraft. Despite severe burns to his arms, hands, neck, shoulder and face, Lt Col Jones attempted to transmit the location of the downed pilot and the enemy gun position to the other aircraft in the area.

However, his radio was disabled so, completely disregarding his injuries, he elected to fly his crippled aircraft back to base and pass on essential information for the rescue rather than bale out. The downed pilot was rescued later in the day.

# WITHDRAWAL AND SECRET MISSIONS

An AC-130A Spectre gunship of the 16th Special Operations Squadron at Ubon in March 1969. The two 20mm Vulcan cannon can be seen forward of the wing *(USAF Museum)*

## In a year that saw US troop strengths down to 474,000, the new President had no qualms about authorising secret strikes

The start of 1969 saw the US forces in Vietnam reach a peak of 365,600 Army personnel and 176,800 from other services.

Most of the fighting would now be against regular North Vietnamese Army (NVA) units, following the decimation of the Viet Cong during the Tet Offensive. The cessation of the bombing campaign over the North now allowed the free movement of supplies all the way from the Haiphong docks to the border with Laos, where they would then follow the Trail to the South.

However, the year would get off to a bad start for the Americans when, on January 14, the USS *Enterprise* suffered a major fire. The carrier was participating in an exercise off Hawaii, prior to returning to Vietnam, when a Zuni rocket on a Phantom was ignited accidentally during start-up procedures. The rocket exploded among the tightly packed aircraft on the deck and the resulting fire took three hours to bring under control. By then 28 men were dead and 15 aircraft were destroyed. Major repairs were necessary at Pearl Harbour, delaying the carrier's arrival at Yankee Station until October 8.

The USS *Enterprise* was participating in an exercise off Hawaii, prior to returning to Vietnam, when a Zuni rocket on a Phantom was ignited accidentally during start-up procedures. The rocket exploded among the tightly packed aircraft on the deck and the resulting fire took three hours to bring under control

### Increasing casualties

Richard Nixon was sworn in as the 37th President of the United States on January 20 and within a month the North Vietnamese decided to test his resolve. On February 23 they launched a nationwide offensive and although it was smaller than the previous year's Tet campaign, US casualties began to increase.

General Abrams (who had succeeded Westmoreland as USMACV) requested authority to bomb the enemy sanctuaries in Cambodia using B-52s and he was probably not a little surprised when Nixon gave his approval.

However, in order to prevent more domestic dissent, the President directed that Operation *Breakfast* be a closely guarded secret and even the B-52 crews were kept in the dark about their targets and bombing to Combat Skyspot instructions. During the next 14 months the B-52s flew 3,630 sorties against targets in Cambodia, dropping over 100,000 tons of bombs in what collectively came to be known as Operation *Menu*.

The US Marine Corps received their first four AH-1G Cobras on April 10, when they arrived at Marble Mountain to join VMO-2's eight UH-1Es and 23 OV-10 Broncos. By

## MEDAL OF HONOR

**John L Levitow – February 24, 1969**

Airman First Class John L Levitow was awarded the Medal of Honor for diving on top of an ignited flare to eject it from his AC-47 Spooky gunship, saving the entire crew on board.

Trained as a loadmaster, Levitow was asked to fill in for the regular loadmaster on an armed AC-47, with the responsibility to set the ejection and ignition timer controls on magnesium flares and pass them to the gunner for deployment.

On the night of February 24 'Spooky 71' was flying night missions near the Tan Son Nhut Air Base area. Levitow was passing flares (which burned at 4,000 degrees) to the gunner when a Viet Cong mortar shell hit the aircraft's right wing and exploded, raking the fuselage with flying shrapnel. Everyone was wounded, including Levitow, and the blast also jarred a flare loose, pulling the safety pin from the canister and arming the fuse.

Although stunned by concussion Levitow saw the smoking flare amid ammunition cans that contained 19,000 rounds of live ammunition. The aircraft was partially out of control and the flare was rolling wildly from side to side. Despite the loss of blood from his many wounds, Levitow threw himself upon the burning flare, hugging the deadly device to his body as he dragged himself to the rear of the aircraft and hurled it through the open cargo door. At that instant the flare separated and ignited in the air, but clear of the aircraft.

**When Nixon became President he authorised the secret bombing of enemy bases in Cambodia. Over 100,000 tons of bombs were dropped by B-52s during Operation *Menu***

**A total of 54 A-37Bs were delivered to the VNAF's 516th, 520th and 524th Fighter Squadrons and as more units converted to the type, the Dragonfly became South Vietnam's principal strike aircraft. Here, South Vietnamese pilots learn from an armourer how to fuse the bomb'**

**This Cessna A-37B Dragonfly made made an emergency landing on a foam-covered runway after ground fire damage resulted in the nose wheel failing to extend. Unusually the pilot has not jettisoned his bomb load prior to attempting the landing**

**The Phantoms of the 12th Tactical Fighter Wing were resident at Cam Ranh Bay from the end of 1965 until the base was closed in March 1971**

**In 1969 a refined Low Light Television (LLTV) system fitted to UH-1H gunships was evaluated in Vietnam. The Iroquis Night Fighter and Night Tracker system (INFANT) was eventually fitted to four platoons of gunships**

**This Royal Australian Air Force Huey was painted in festive markings to celebrate Christmas 1969 in Vietnam. Note the winch by the cargo door**

the end of the year the squadron was at its full strength of 24 AH-1Gs and was pleased with its "far-superior weapons platform", compared to the UH-1E.

The one main complaint that the Marines did have though, was that the AH-1G only had one engine and with the amount of time that Marine helicopters spent at sea, two engines would be preferable. The Marines eventually procured the twin-engined AH-1J Sea Cobra and the first of these arrived in Vietnam for combat evaluation two years later.

By the summer of 1969 Nixon's policy of Vietnamisation' was underway. Three 'Vietnamese Air Force (VNAF) squadrons had retired their piston-powered Skyraiders and converted to the Cessna A-37 Dragonfly ground-attack jets by July.

A total of 54 A-37Bs were delivered to the VNAF's 516th, 520th and 524th Fighter Squadrons and as more units converted to the type, the Dragonfly became South Vietnam's principal strike aircraft.

## Withdrawals & releases

President Nixon met Nguyen Van Thieu (South Vietnam's President since 1967) at Midway Island on June 18 to discuss the war, and the first withdrawal of 25,000 US servicemen was announced.

On July 18, the North Vietnamese released three US prisoners of war into the hands of an American anti-war group in Hanoi. The North Vietnamese warned the POWs not to cause them any 'embarrassment' or they would retaliate against those left behind.

However, the other POWs had urged the trio to speak out about their ill-treatment and at a press conference on September 3 Navy Lieutenant Robert F Frishman did just that. He announced that the POWs had been beaten, tortured, placed in solitary confinement, provided minimal medical care and otherwise mistreated.

Ten days later at the International Conference of the Red Cross meeting in Istanbul, Turkey, the US government, which had in fact known about the torture for at least two years, finally reported Hanoi's gross violations of the Geneva Convention. The same day that Frishman held his press conference, Ho Chi Minh died in Hanoi, and a three-day cease fire was observed in his honour. From then on the treatment of the prisoners of war began to improve.

The first round of US troop withdrawals was completed by the end of August and on September 16 Nixon announced that 35,000 more troops would leave Vietnam by the end of the year.

Meanwhile, the North Vietnamese had not made any concessions as a result of the troop withdrawals and continued to drag their feet at peace talks. Back in Washington DC, one quarter of a million anti-war protesters invaded the city's streets in October – the fate of the war was being decided not in Vietnam, but on the streets of the USA.

**F-100D Super Sabre 56-3456 at Tuy Hoa air base in 1969** *(USAF Museum)*

**In October the 44th TFS moved its F-105s from the Phantom-equipped 388th TFW at Korat to join the 355th TFW at Takhli, thus consolidating all Southeast Asia Thunderchief assets at one base** *(USAF Museum)*

## MEDAL OF HONOR

**Michael J Novosel – October 2, 1969**

Medevac UH-1 Huey pilot Michael J Novosel was awarded the Medal of Honor for the rescue of 29 US and South Vietnamese Army soldiers from a heavily fortified enemy training area.

Novosel had served in both the World War Two and the Korean War and was on his second tour of Vietnam. On the morning of October 2, 1969, he set out to evacuate a group of soldiers who were surrounded by the enemy near the Cambodian border. Without air cover or fire support, Novosel flew at low altitude under continuous enemy fire. He skimmed the ground while his medic and crew chief yanked the wounded men on board. He completed 15 hazardous extractions, was wounded in a barrage of enemy fire and momentarily lost control of his helicopter, but when it was over, he had rescued 29 men.

## VNAF expansion

As plans were being drawn up to expand the VNAF by 1,100 aircraft and helicopters, the slow withdrawal of USAF squadrons began. The 8th Tactical Bomb Squadron flew its B-57 Canberras back to the USA for storage on October 6. The unit, along with the 13th TBS, were among the first squadrons to deploy to Vietnam in August 1964. Only one in three of the 96 B-57s assigned to the two squadrons survived to return to the States.

In October the 44th TFS moved its F-105s from the Phantom-equipped 388th TFW at Korat to join the 355th TFW at Takhli, thus consolidating all Southeast Asia Thunderchief assets at one base. The USAF presence at Pleiku and Binh Thuy was reduced to one squadron at each and Nha Trang Air Base was turned over to the VNAF.

The withdrawal continued in November and December with the 41st Tactical Electronic Warfare Squadron at Takhli RTAFB deactivating and redistributing its 15 EB-66C Destroyers among other units. The F-102 detachments at Udorn and Da Nang were withdrawn and the 609th SOS at Nakhon Phanom returned its A-26A Invaders to the USA for storage. The last AC-47 squadron, the 4th SOS, deactivated and gave its gunships to the VNAF. Three were retained for base defence and others were given to the Air Forces of Thailand, Laos and Cambodia.

**The North Vietnamese Air Force was equipped with a small number of the MiG-19 *Farmer* fighters. Pictured here are MiG-19 pilots discussing tactics on their flightline** *(USAF Museum)*

With US troop strength already down to 474,000, President Nixon announced in December that 50,000 more were to be withdrawn over the next four months. Thailand also announced plans to withdraw its 12,000-man contingent, although the 50,000 South Korean troops were to remain for the time being.

Despite the fact that most large Viet Cong and NVA regular units had withdrawn to their sanctuaries in Laos and Cambodia, US losses for 1969 stood at 9,249 dead, 69,043 wounded and 112 missing. During the year 132,000 communists were claimed to have been killed, although 115,000 replacements had been infiltrated south at the same time. By the end of 1969 though, combat activity was at its lowest level since 1964. ❖

# TAKING THE FIGHT TO CAMBODIA

Helicopter gunships found many lucrative targets inside Cambodia, including enemy barracks and formations of troops in the open

## Despite a shrinking force of aircraft and personnel, the US continued to take the fight to the enemy, and made a daring raid to rescue American prisoners

The new decade saw continued base reductions in South Vietnam and Thailand, and by the end of the year the USAF would move completely out of Binh Thuy, Pleiku, Tuy Hoa and Vung Tau in South Vietnam and Don Muang airport and Takhli in Thailand.

However, the intensification of the air campaign against the Ho Chi Minh Trail through Laos caused the North Vietnamese to seek alternative supply routes through Cambodia.

Communist ships began using the port of Sihanoukville to unload supplies, which were then trucked to the supply bases along the South Vietnamese border. By the previous summer enough supplies had been getting through to support enemy activities in two-thirds of Vietnam and around 40,000 Viet Cong and NVA troops were in Cambodia, supplying arms and ammunition to the local communist Khmer Rouge insurgents.

Prince Norodom Sihanouk had managed to keep his nation out of the conflict so far, by turning a blind eye to both American bombers and North Vietnamese supply convoys, but on March 18 that came to an end.

General Lon Nol, the pro-Western army chief of staff ousted Prince Sihanouk, closed the port of Sihanoukville and ordered the North Vietnamese out of the country. Fighting soon broke out between the North Vietnamese and the weak Cambodian Army.

### A demonstration of resolve

President Nixon was convinced that the North Vietnamese would not negotiate seriously until they accepted that America could defeat them on the battlefield and he believed that the time was right for a demonstration of his resolve.

US General Abrams asked for tactical air strikes to be used against the NVA in Cambodia – in addition to the Operation *Menu* B-52 strikes – and on April 24 Operation *Patio* began when the President approved a cross-border offensive against the enemy sanctuaries in Cambodia.

On April 29, the South Vietnamese Army attacked the sanctuaries in the Parrot's Beak area and two days later the US Army's 1st Cavalry Division also launched an airmobile assault into the Fishhook region – helicopter gunships having a field day decimating enemy formations caught in the open, supposedly safe in their sanctuaries. Tactical aircraft, B-52 bombers and fixed-wing gunships flew in support of the Army of the Republic of Vietnam (ARVN) and US ground forces and USAF C-130s also flew 21 *Commando Vault* missions in which they rolled 15,000lb *Daisy Cutter* bombs out of their rear cargo doors to blast enemy positions or create instant helicopter landing zones in the jungle.

The campaign was a resounding success in the short term, with the capture of thousands of tons of enemy rice, millions of rounds of ammunition and an estimated enemy casualty figure of 4,800 killed. It was a major setback to the North Vietnamese and led to the reduction of US fatalities in South Vietnam over the following six months from 93 to 51 per week.

In the long term, however, the invasion provoked a serious backlash of public opinion in the USA. Violent student demonstrations on college campuses came to a head at Kent State in Ohio, where four demonstrators were shot dead by National Guardsmen.

An anxious Senate passed the Cooper-Church amendment, which prohibited the use of American ground troops in Cambodia or Laos after June 30 and

The *Tropic Moon* B-57Gs were equipped with forward-looking radar, infrared and LLTV, plus a laser device. They were used for night and all-weather bombing missions over the Ho Chi Minh Trail and it is claimed that their accuracy was such that 80% of their bombs hit within 15ft of their aiming point

## MEDAL OF HONOR

**Raymond M Clausen Jr – December 31, 1970**

Private Raymond M Clausen Jr was awarded the Medal of Honor after risking his life to rescue several Marines from a minefield.

Clausen was on his second tour of duty with Marine Medium Helicopter Squadron HMM-263 and on January 31, 1970 he was participating in a helicopter rescue mission to extract elements of a platoon which had inadvertently entered a minefield while attacking enemy positions. He skilfully guided the helicopter pilot to a landing in an area cleared by one of several mine explosions. With eleven Marines wounded, one dead, and the remaining eight Marines holding their positions for fear of detonating other mines, Clausen leaped from the helicopter and, in the face of enemy fire, moved across the extremely hazardous, mine-laden area to assist in carrying several casualties to the waiting helicopter. Only when he was certain that all Marines were safely aboard did he signal the pilot to lift the helicopter.

On June 15, 1971, Clausen was presented the Medal of Honor by President Richard Nixon in a ceremony at the White House.

> “The invasion provoked a serious backlash of public opinion in the USA”

Oops! This C-47 from the 9th SOS ‘came a cropper’ at Bien Hoa in May 1970

There were now over 500 American prisoners of war located in various prisons in North Vietnam. Fifty were held at Son Tay prison and in 1970 a plan was formulated to rescue the prisoners them. The HH-53s landed outside the prison compound and, after breaching the walls, the Rangers began systematically clearing of the cellblocks. Within minutes they realised that the cells were empty; the prisoners had been moved to another prison and US intelligence had not detected the move

the US Army had no alternative but to withdraw.

The air strikes continued though via Operation *Freedom Deal* and 8,000 sorties were flown in Cambodia up to February 1971. Over 40% of the sorties would be against targets outside the authorised area of operations.

## *Tropic Moon III*

The 13th TBS returned to Southeast Asia on September 15 and brought with them eleven *Tropic Moon III* B-57G Night Intruder aircraft. They were based at Ubon and became part of the veteran 8th TFW, which had recently flown its 100,000th sortie.

The *Tropic Moon* B-57Gs were equipped with forward-looking radar, infra-red and LLTV, plus a laser device. They were used for night and all-weather bombing missions over the Ho Chi Minh Trail and it is claimed that their accuracy was such that 80% of their bombs hit within 15ft of their aiming point. They returned home in April 1972, having lost only one aircraft (in a mid-air collision with an O-2A FAC in the darkness of southern Laos in December 1970).

Any USAF units not actively engaged in combat operations in Vietnam began withdrawing from Thailand from October through Project *Banner Sun*. The main unit to be affected was the F-105 equipped 355th TFW at Takhli, which ceased combat operations on October 7. Soon the only F-105s left in Thailand were the *Wild Weasels* of the 17th WWS at Korat, which would remain until October 1974. The Thunderchief fleet had suffered heavy losses over the years; 344 had been lost in combat, together with 63 to other causes.

The 1st Cavalry Division created 'Pink Teams' of an OH-6A Loach and an AH-1G working together to seek and destroy the enemy

Other squadrons going home were the 22nd and 602nd SOS (which redistributed its Skyraiders to various units before deactivating). They were joined by the 45th TRS which had first deployed its RF-101C Voodoos to Vietnam in November 1961. They left Tan Son Nhut for Mississippi on November 16 and had lost 39 aircraft over their nine-year deployment.

After three and a half years of combat operations, the Royal Australian Air Force's 2 Sqn lost its first Canberra bomber on November 3. Magpie 91 was on a *Combat Skyspot* mission in the Da Nang area and released its bomb load at 22,000ft. The radar bombing operator was still in contact with the aircraft when its pilot reported that he was turning on a heading of 120 degrees. That was the last transmission received from the two-man crew. Despite an extensive search, no sign was ever found of the missing aircraft.

> "Over 40% of the sorties would be against targets outside the authorised area of operations"

**US General Abrams asked for tactical air strikes to be used against the NVA in Cambodia – in addition to the Operation *Menu* B-52 strikes – and on April 24 Operation *Patio* began when the President approved a cross-border offensive against the enemy sanctuaries in Cambodia**

## Son Tay raid

There were now over 500 American prisoners of war located in various prisons throughout North Vietnam. Fifty were held at Son Tay prison, 28 miles northwest of Hanoi and in June 1970 the US Joint Chiefs of Staff (JCS) asked Brigadier General Donald D Blackburn, Special Assistant for Counter-insurgency and Special Activity, to formulate a plan to raid Son Tay and rescue the prisoners.

Just before midnight on November 20, one HH-3E and five HH-53 helicopters carrying 92 Army Rangers took off from Udorn in Thailand. Diversionary attacks were being launched all over North Vietnam while the raiders, flying below 500ft, closed on the prison.

Two *Combat Talon* C-130E 'unconventional warfare aircraft' dropped napalm markers and fire fight simulators on the nearby sapper school, as the HH-3E dropped into the small prison compound. The HH-53s landed outside the compound and after breaching the walls, the Rangers began a systematic clearing of the cell blocks, killing every North Vietnamese guard they met on the way.

Within minutes they realised that the cells were empty; the prisoners had been moved in July to another prison seven miles away and US intelligence had not detected the move. Less than half an hour after they arrived over the prison, the raiders departed.

Despite the intelligence failure, the raid itself was a tactical success and had the prisoners still been there they probably would have been rescued. Furthermore, news of the rescue attempt soon reached the POWs and morale was boosted accordingly. The North Vietnamese were severely shaken by the raid and within days all the POWs in North Vietnam had been moved to two or three prisons in the Hanoi area. The resulting overcrowding of the cells was a blessing in disguise; some prisoners who had been in solitary confinement for five years were ecstatic to find that they now had a cellmate.

**This unofficial badge was later issued to the crews who took part in the daring raid on Son Tay**

Throughout 1970, a total of 171 USAF aircraft had been lost, bringing the total number to 1,950, representing a cost of $2.5 billion.

The number of combat sorties had been reduced substantially from 966,949, to 711,440, of which 30,000 were flown over Cambodia. The Pacific Air Force had been reduced by 19 tactical squadrons, more than 500 aircraft and 32,000 personnel.

In contrast, the Vietnamese Air Force now had 728 aircraft in 30 squadrons and they flew a total of 292,523 sorties in 1970.

**From locations along the borders with Cambodia and Laos, USAF helicopters covertly inserted reconnaissance teams along the Ho Chi Minh Trail** *(USAF Museum)*

As Congress had forbidden the use of American combat troops in Laos, the fighting would have to be carried out by South Vietnamese troops, with US logistical and air support. Estimates put the ARVN losses at 7,000 killed and an unknown number wounded

# CUTTING OFF THE SUPPLY CHAIN

**Offensives to cut off supply routes in Laos and the Ho Chi Minh Trail cost the Allies dearly. And it soon became obvious that Hanoi had no intention of scaling back its offensive**

The previous year's efforts to cut off North Vietnamese supply routes through Cambodia saw activities intensify along the Ho Chi Minh Trail. During the first six weeks of 1971 alone an estimated 31,000 North Vietnamese Army (NVA) troops and 1,800 trucks arrived in Laos. It was obvious that a dry-season offensive into either South Vietnam or Cambodia was being planned, so President Nixon authorised a pre-emptive strike against the enemy bases in Laos.

However, as Congress had prevented the use of American combat troops in Laos, the fighting would have to be carried out by South Vietnamese Army of the Republic of Vietnam (ARVN) troops, with the US providing logistical and air support.

The ARVN forces consisted of three divisions, three Ranger battalions, and an armoured brigade, backed by one US Marine medium transport helicopter squadron, the 2nd Squadron/7th Cavalry, and a number of other aviation units under the operational control of the 101st Aviation Group.

## Lam Son 719

Operation *Lam Son 719* was launched on February 8, with the objective of reaching the major NVA supply base at Tchepone, 22 miles inside Laos.The AVRN vehicle were flanked by infantry units and the airborne assets, while artillery bases were established on the high ground. The invasion force advanced six miles on the first day but the enemy soon reacted violently to the offensive and a month of heavy fighting ensued.

On March 6, two ARVN battalions in 120 VNAF Bell UH-1H helicopters made an air assault into Tchepone and captured the town with only light casualties. By now the over-extended ARVN units were coming under increasingly heavy pressure as NVA reinforcements were committed to battle. The helicopter sorties were also seriously affected by bad weather and when they could fly, they were up against the heaviest anti-aircraft fire of the war.

Lt Gen Hoang Xuan Lam, the ARVN commander, faced with increasing personnel and equipment losses and worsening weather, ordered a fighting withdrawal. Such a manoeuvre is difficult even with well-trained, disciplined troops, and the ARVN losses were heavy with at least 7,000 men dead and an unknown number wounded.

The Americans (who had only been providing air support) losses numbered 176 killed, 1,042 wounded and 42 missing in action. The total of US casualties is unsurprising considering that 107 helicopters were destroyed and over 600 damaged.

Despite the cost of Lam Son 719, the enemy lost around 20,000 tons of food and ammunition, 156,000 gallons of fuel, 1,530 trucks, 74 tanks and 6,000 weapons in the offensive. It also delayed the enemy offensive for a full twelve months and brought Saigon and Washington additional time to carry out the 'Vietnamisation' programme.

Within days of the end of the invasion, President Nixon announced that 100,000 more US troops would be withdrawn by December.

Hovering Huey helicopters pour machine gun fire into a treeline to cover the advance of South Vietnamese ground troops

## SAMs in Laos

With US air activity over North Vietnam largely confined to armed reconnaissance flights and the occasional reprisal raid and with a slackening of air support requirements in the South – due to the reduction in the level of fighting – attention could be focused on the Ho Chi Minh Trail.

However, the cessation of the *Rolling Thunder* campaign meant that the North Vietnamese had plenty of anti-aircraft weapons to spare and the presence of the first surface-to-air missile (SAM) site in Laos was confirmed on March 4. On April 26, an O-2 FAC aircraft flying in the area became the first US aircraft lost to a SAM over Laos.

During the monsoon season in Laos, the North Vietnamese managed to build 140 miles of new road on the Ho Chi Minh Trail, bringing the total distance of routes to a staggering 2,170 miles. By the end of the year, 344 anti-aircraft guns and thousands of smaller automatic weapons defended vital points along the Ho Chi Minh Trail. More SAM sites were constructed in Laos and on the Vietnamese border and by rebuilding their air bases in southern North Vietnam, NVA MiGs could challenge the dwindling USAF operations.

## More withdrawals

In June 1971 the last USAF O-1 Bird Dogs were transferred to the VNAF. Since their arrival in Vietnam, they had flown over 471,000 sorties. On July 30 the final F-100 Super Sabres departed for the USA, the fleet amassing 360,283 sorties since their arrival in 1964 – for the loss of 243 aircraft.

The number of US bases in South Vietnam continued to reduce as units returned to the USA or relocated to Thailand. Bien Hoa was handed over to the VNAF in August and Phu Cat followed in December, leaving only Da Nang, Cam Ranh Bay, Phan Rang and Tan Son Nhut.

With the onset of the dry season late

## MEDAL OF HONOR

**William Adams – May 25, 1971**

Major William Adams was awarded the Medal of Honor posthumously for trying to rescue three wounded men in his UH-1H helicopter.

Serving with the US Army's 227th Assault Helicopter Company, 52nd Aviation Battalion in Kontum Province, Adams volunteered to fly a lightly armed helicopter in an attempt to evacuate three seriously wounded soldiers from a small base that was under attack by a large enemy force. He was aware that anti-aircraft weapons were positioned around the base and that the clear weather would afford the enemy gunners unobstructed views of all routes into the base. As he approached the area the enemy engaged but Adams directed the fire of his supporting gunships as he continued his approach to the base. He landed and calmly waited until the wounded soldiers were placed on board. As his aircraft departed it was struck by anti-aircraft fire and exploded, plummeting to earth amid the hail of enemy fire

“The USAF was still bearing the brunt of the air war”

**In June 1971 the last USAF O-1 Bird Dogs were transferred to the VNAF. Since their arrival in Vietnam they had flown over 471,000 sorties**

**Although the South Vietnamese troops captured many enemy weapons during Operation *Lam Son 719*, they suffered heavy casualties as they withdrew**

**An F-5 Tiger II is transitioned to South Vietnam as part of the Nixon Administration’s ’Vietnamisation’ policy, which was designed to hand American combat roles to South Vietnamese troops while US troops pulled out of the war** *(USAF Museum)*

in the year, the enemy strength in Laos and Cambodia began to increase. On December 10, President Nixon warned Hanoi that North Vietnam would be bombed if it increased the level of fighting as US troops were withdrawn from the South. Within a couple of months, events were to prove that, if they were indeed listening, the leaders in Hanoi paid very little attention to the President’s warning.

## Reconnaissance

Although the bombing campaign over North Vietnam had effectively come to a halt over three years before, reconnaissance flights still kept an eye on the enemy’s progress. Lockheed U-2 and SR-71 spyplanes and tactical reconnaissance aircraft such as the USAF’s RF-4C Phantom and RF-101 Voodoo as well as US Navy RF-8 Crusaders and RA-5C Vigilantes provided daily updates to the overall intelligence picture.

It soon became obvious that North Vietnam was stockpiling supplies, weapons and ammunition and increasing the number of men moving South, in preparation for a major offensive.

Although safe passage for the reconnaissance flights had been theoretically agreed at Peace Talks in Paris, the North Vietnamese continued to fire on them. In the last three weeks of 1971, ten US aircraft had been shot down over North Vietnam and Laos and in retaliation (and in an attempt to deter Hanoi from launching an offensive in 1972) President Nixon authorised Operation *Proud Deep*, the largest series of air strikes against the North since 1968.

For five days from December 26, the American aircraft flew 1,025 sorties against enemy airfields, SAM sites, fuel storage areas, supply dumps and truck parks below the 20th Parallel. The North Vietnamese were undeterred; soon their long-range artillery began shelling ARVN outposts across the demilitarised zone (DMZ).

Meanwhile, the improvement and modernisation programme for the VNAF continued at full speed and by the end of 1971 the VNAF had 1,202 aircraft and 1,109 aircrew. During the year it had flown 524,000 sorties and had lost 57 aircraft.

However, only 59,800 of those VNAF flights were actual combat sorties and the USAF was still bearing the brunt of the air war. It flew 450,000 combat sorties during the year, losing 87 aircraft.

The KC-135 tanker fleet alone performed 62,500 aerial refuellings and the tactical airlift system moved 2,282,000 passengers and 283,000 tons of cargo, despite the run-down of American strength.

At the end of 1971, American military strength had declined to 156,800 and Australia, New Zealand and South Korea had all announced that their troops were to leave. ❖

# SNATCHING DEFEAT FROM THE JAWS OF VICTORY

The 129 B-52 bombers arrived in three waves, four to five hours apart and attacked the airfields at Hoa Lac, Kep and Phuc Yen, the Kinh No complex and the Yen Vien railyards *(USAF Museum)*

**With North Vietnamese massing at the border and ready to invade, there wasn't much the rapidly depleted US forces could do to fend them off. It was time to call in reinforcements**

In the first three months of 1972 Operation Proud Deep, which took place against the North Vietnamese in late 1971, was followed up by 90 further raids. Reconnaissance flights also continued and on January 19, while flying MiG CAP for a reconnaissance mission over Quang Lang airfield, Lts Cunningham and Driscoll, flying an F-4J Phantom off the USS Constellation shot down a MiG-21 *Fishbed*. It was the US Navy's first MiG kill in 18 months. The USAF, however, would have to wait until February 21 before an F-4D claimed a MiG-21 shot down; this being the first USAF MiG kill in more than four years.

## Massing hordes

By the end of February, ten of North Vietnam's 13 Divisions were poised to invade South Vietnam. Three were north of the demilitarised zone (opposite Quang Tri province in northern Military Region I) and one had infiltrated into the A Shau Valley, south of the DMZ.

Two were in Laos (opposite Military Region II) and another had infiltrated through to Binh Dinh province near the coast. A further three were in Cambodia, preparing to cross into Binh Long and Tay Ninh provinces, a mere 60 miles north of Saigon.

Not much could be done to counter the enemy's invasion preparations because of the rundown of US air power in South Vietnam. The last US Marine Corps aircraft had left in 1971, most of the air bases had been handed over to the Vietnamese Air Force (VNAF) and only two aircraft carriers were now present at Yankee Station. A single USAF squadron of A-37s remained at Bien Hoa and three Phantom squadrons and five AC-119Ks were still at Da Nang.

Some Marine and Army helicopter units were still in-country but most of the American combat troops had left Vietnam and, on the whole, South Vietnam was on its own. All leave was cancelled, the recruit training programme was accelerated and forces were positioned to meet the anticipated attack.

## Imminent invasion

The invasion began on March 30, 1972 when, under the cover of very low cloud ceilings and low visibility, 30,000 North Vietnamese troops, together with two regiments of tanks thrust into Quang Tri Province. The attack was co-ordinated with similar thrusts toward Loc Ninh and An Loc and from Laos towards Dak To, Kontum and Pleiku in the Central Highlands.

The Army of the Republic of Vietnam (ARVN) defenders faced ground assaults, backed by masses of artillery and for the first time PT-76 and T-54 tanks. The weather was so bad that air support was limited and what did get through found itself opposed by very heavy anti-aircraft fire. Mobile surface-to-air (SAM) sites soon appeared in the South, together with the new shoulder-fired SA-7 Strela heat-seeking anti-aircraft missile, effective up to 8,000ft.

The attacks left the ARVN defenders reeling and they began to lose ground as

This F-4J Phantom is from Navy Fighter Squadron VF-142 'Ghostriders' flying from the USS Constellation. During their seven deployments they shot down five enemy aircraft making the squadron the Navy's first 'Ace Squadron' of the war

◄ Lockheed C-130A-45-LM Hercules 57-0460 of the South Vietnamese Air Force. The aircraft served with the VNAF from October 1972 to April 1975. During the fall of Saigon, it was flown from Tan Son Nhut Air Base to Singapore, carrying about 350 Vietnamese. Returned to USAF service in August 1975, it was assigned to the 16th Special Operations Squadron at Korat Royal Thai Air Force Base, Thailand, then used by the USAF Air National Guard for many years, before being retired in 1989. Today, this aircraft is part of the National Air and Space Museum, given its historic past *(USAF Museum)*

their American advisers tried to call in air strikes or direct artillery support from US warships offshore.

## Reinforcements

The day after the invasion started, the USAF's 35th Tactical Fighter Squadron (TFS) at Kunsan in South Korea was ordered to fly its F-4Ds to Da Nang, to reinforce the 366th Tactical Fighter Wing (TFW), which was still in residence there. The Marines were hot on their heels and two Phantom squadrons began deploying to Da Nang from Japan on April 6. A third squadron followed on April 13, together with a detachment of EA-6A Prowlers for ECM missions and two TA-4F Skyhawks to perform airborne spotting of naval gunfire for ships of the Seventh Fleet.

Finally, in mid-May, two Skyhawk squadrons arrived at Bien Hoa to join in the defence of An Loc. One of the squadrons was VA-311, the last Marine fixed-wing unit to have left Vietnam – almost exactly a year earlier.

The Navy also reinforced its two aircraft carriers on Yankee Station with the USS *Constellation* and USS *Kitty Hawk* arriving by April 8 and had ordered the USS *Midway* and USS *Saratoga* to join them. By late spring, six carriers, each with an air wing of 90 aircraft, were in action; the greatest number of the war.

## *Constant Guard*

Back in the US, the Tactical Air Command initiated a series of major deployments, known as *Constant Guard I-IV*.

*Constant Guard I* saw the despatch of the 561st TFS and its F-105G *Wild Weasels* to Korat where they joined eight EB-66 Destroyers from Shaw AFB. The 334th and 336th TFS followed with their F-4Es and all 36 aircraft were at Ubon by April 12.

On May 1, *Constant Guard II* began and involved the transfer of the 58th and 308th TFS to Udorn with their 36 F-4Es.

*Constant Guard III* became the largest single move in the history of Tactical Air Command. On May 7, the 49th TFW began to deploy its four Phantom squadrons to Takhli and was soon flying ground-support missions around An Loc and Kontum. Some 36 C-130E Hercules transport aircraft from the 36th and 61st Tactical Airlift Squadrons followed next, under *Constant Guard IV*.

Strategic Air Command began a series of deployments of B-52D and G bombers to Andersen AFB on Guam during April and May under the codenames *Bullet Shot I-V*. Some bombers were flying missions over Vietnam less than 72 hours after receiving deployment alert at their stateside bases and by May 30, some 117 B-52s were on Guam.

# “The first USAF MiG kill in more than four years”

**Ninety retaliatory raids were flown against North Vietnam during the first three months of 1972, compared to only 108 during all of 1971**

**On January 19, 1972, while flying MiG CAP for a reconnaissance mission over Quang Lang airfield, Lts Cunningham and Driscoll, flying an F-4J Phantom off the USS Constellation made the Navy's first MiG kill in 18 months when they shot down a MiG-21**

**◄ This Soviet-made, high-altitude helmet was worn by some North Vietnamese MiG-21 pilots during the latter years of the war** *(USAF Museum)*

**► Six UH-1Ms armed with the SS-11 missile were in action during the Easter invasion. However, the XM-22 SS-11 system was a far more difficult system to operate than the TOW XM-26 system, which was almost five times more effective** *(Robert N Steinbrunn via Phil Chinnery)*

The B-52 was the only aircraft that could still bomb in all weathers during the first few days of the invasion. In the first week, B-52s flew 132 missions and on April 9 they resumed bombing strikes against targets north of the demilitarised zone.

By May 30, the USAF Order of Battle in South Vietnam and Thailand consisted of 20 A-1 Skyraiders, 20 A-37s, 54 B-52s, 14 AC-119s, 14 AC-130s, 348 F-4s and 31 F-105s.

## Bending the rules

Despite President Nixon's strong action following the invasion, the previous restrictions had still not been thrown out of the window. On April 11, General John W Vogt Jr, relieved General John D Lavelle as Commander, Seventh Air Force. General Lavelle had been accused of bending the rules of engagement and ordering protective reaction strikes against enemy anti-aircraft artillery (AAA) sites, ignoring the requirement from Washington that the AAA were supposed to fire at the US aircraft first.

Reports on some of the strikes had been falsified and one of the intelligence specialists of the 432nd TRW complained to his Senator about it, thus bringing about an enquiry. The incident was a prime example of the stupidity of the rules of engagement, in which a pilot could not hit a SAM site until it showed hostile intent and launched a missile at him. Within a few weeks the enemy offensive was in full swing and US bombers began destroying the same targets that Lavelle had been sacked for hitting.

## Advancing

When the weather improved, airstrikes managed to stall the enemy advance, but by May 2 the North Vietnamese had captured Quang Tri City.

Elsewhere, Loc Ninh was overrun by the 5th Viet Cong/NVA Division, while two more Divisions converged on An Loc. The enemy attacked the city on the May 13, but the ARVN defenders, supported by AH-1G Cobras from the US Army's 3rd Brigade, 1st Cavalry Division and intense air strikes, repulsed the attack.

A second attack two days later was also halted, so the communists decided to lay siege to the city and starve the defenders instead. Both Region III airfields were out of action and the only method of resupplying the defenders was by airdrop from C-130s – despite the AAA in the region.

In Military Region II, two North Vietnamese Divisions attacked across the border from Laos and by April 24 they had captured Dak To. A third division had infiltrated across country to the coastal region of Binh Dinh Province, east of

## MEDAL OF HONOR

**Steve Bennett – June 29, 1972**

OV-10 Forward Air Controller Capt Steve Bennett was awarded the Medal of Honour posthumously after ditching his aircraft in the sea following battle damage.

A forward air controller (FAC) assigned to the 20th Tactical Air Support Squadron, Bennett (and his back-seater – Capt Michael B. Brown) was flying his OV-10 Bronco on an artillery adjustment mission southeast of Quang Tri City when a ground artillery spotter with a platoon of South Vietnamese marines radioed for help because they were being overrun by NVA regulars.

Brown could not call in artillery fire without hitting the South Vietnamese troops so, at great personal risk, he decided to attack the NVA troops with the Bronco’s machine guns. After four strafing attacks he had forced the NVA to retreat, and his OV-10 had received only slight damage from ground fire. However, on Bennett’s fifth attack the OV-10’s left engine was hit by an SA-7 heat-seeking missile. Another FAC pilot warned Bennett to eject but shrapnel had destroyed Brown’s parachute and Bennett refused to leave him behind.

Therefore, Bennett decided to ditch his aircraft in the nearby Tonkin Gulf. Upon hitting the water, the OV-10 flipped over, and the front cockpit broke apart. Brown managed to free himself from the wreckage, but he could not help Bennett.

**Captain Roger Locher spent 23 days evading the enemy on the ground before he was picked up by a combat rescue team**

**B-52 crewmen being briefed on their next mission: Hanoi**

Pleiku. They captured several coastal towns and blocked the north-south coastal road before B-52 strikes stopped the drive short of Qui Nhon.

Following the fall of Dak To, the highways to Kontum were cut and two months of heavy fighting ensued while the city was supplied by air. The first major battle of Kontum occurred on May 14, but was broken up by fighter strikes and three UH-1B gunships equipped with the new tube-launched, optical-tracked, wire-guided (TOW) anti-tank missiles. The TOW missiles were undergoing field trials and happened to be in the right place at the right time. By June 12, TOW-equipped UH-1Bs had destroyed 26 enemy tanks.

As the fighting continued, President Nixon prepared to carry out the threat he had made in December. On May 8 he went on TV and announced that he intended to cut off the flow of supplies that had for so long, permitted Hanoi to continue its war in the South.

The new campaign was named *Linebacker I* and commenced with Operation *Pocket Money* on May 9. On that day three A-6 Intruders and six A-7 Corsairs from the Coral Sea shrieked across Haiphong harbour at 50ft, released four 2,000lb mines each and escaped without a scratch.

**Boeing B-52D Stratofortresses on the ramp at Anderson AFB on Guam**

The mining of the North Vietnamese ports had a devastating effect on the communist war effort; 85% of the country’s imports and all of its oil arrived through Haiphong. With the ports closed, the only other supply lines into the country were the railroads and eight major highways into China. These would all come under attack in September when Operation *Prime Choke* was launched against the railroad bridges in the buffer zone between the North and China.

### *Linebacker*

On May 10, three and a half years after President Johnson called a halt to the *Rolling Thunder* campaign, full-scale bombing operations over North Vietnam resumed. The *Linebacker* campaign was different from the *Rolling Thunder* campaign in a number of ways. For the first time, the President was prepared to risk the wrath of the Soviets and Chinese, by attempting to isolate North Vietnam from external supply. He relaxed the

**An F-4D from 555th 'Triple Nickel' Tactical Fighter Squadron of the 8th Tactical Fighter Wing releases an Mk84 laser guided bomb over North Vietnam**

**Target Hanoi – an aerial photograph of the city taken after the bombing campaign to prove that indiscriminate carpet bombing did not take place**

**Sixty more B-52s attacked Hanoi on December 28 and 29. The few SAMs that were launched exploded harmlessly away from the bombers and all returned safely**

rules of engagement and gave the local commanders more latitude and flexibility in directing the air operations than before. Improved munitions were also now available, including Laser Guided Bombs (LGBs), which now meant that difficult targets could now be struck with precision. Lastly, President Nixon had the will to win and he wanted results.

The air battles of May 10 merit a book unto themselves. The 32 Phantoms from the 8th TFW at Ubon flew North; 16 were loaded with unguided 'iron bombs' and heading for the Yen Vien railyard north of Hanoi and the other 16, loaded with the new 'smart' bombs, were about to pay a visit to the Paul Doumer Bridge.

Because of the extent of the air defences over North Vietnam, the strike aircraft were outnumbered by support aircraft. Eight Phantoms were to provide ECM chaff support, 15 F-105G *Wild Weasels* were along to handle SAM suppression and four EB-66s would orbit for ECM jamming. MiG CAP would be provided by Phantoms from the 555th *Triple Nickel* TFS.

During the mission, 160 SAMs were fired at the strike force, but the attack was carried out successfully and one span of the bridge dropped into the river. To the enemy's surprise, a second strike force returned the following day and dropped a further three spans, closing the bridge for the duration of the war.

## MiG action

The four Phantoms from *Triple Nickel's* Oyster Flight ran into four of the 41 MiG-21s launched that day – and despatched three of them in short order. Suddenly, four more appeared and caught Oyster One, flown by Maj Robert Lodge and Capt Roger Locher, in a stream of cannon fire. Lodge died as his aircraft exploded, but Locher ejected safely and landed deep inside North Vietnam, where he evaded capture for an amazing 23 days until a combat rescue team brought him out.

While the raid on the Paul Doumer bridge was going on, a strike force of Navy A-6 Intruders and A-7 Corsairs hit the Hai Duong railyard between Hanoi and Haiphong. Here, 22 MiGs engaged the strike force and their Phantom escorts and in the ensuing melee, seven North Vietnamese Air Force (NVAF) *Fishbeds* were shot down.

Three were claimed by Lts Cunningham and Driscoll, who already had two kills to their credit, but as their fuel ran low and they headed toward the Gulf, they were hit by a SAM missile over Haiphong and had to eject over the water. They were rescued by helicopter and returned to the USS *Constellation* where they were feted as the first American air aces of the Vietnam War.

## Dam-busting

LGBs were used with great effect again on June 10 when the 8th TFW was finally given permission to attack the Soviet-built Lang Chi hydro-electric plant on the Red River. The plant was capable of supplying 75% of North Vietnam's electricity, but breaching the dam would have meant drowning 23,000 civilians.

Three flights of Phantoms with 2000lb LGBs carried out the attack; the first blowing the roof off. The second flight missed its target (the transformer yard) but the last flight put all of its bombs into the roofless plant, destroying the turbines and generators without putting even a crack in the dam.

By the end of June more than 100 bridges in North Vietnam had been destroyed, together with all the major fuel tank farms and the pipeline running south to the DMZ.

The invasion in the South had ground to a halt, largely due to the application of US air power, especially the B-52 bombers. The sieges of An Loc and Kontum had been lifted, although Quang Tri would not be retaken again until September.

## MEDAL OF HONOR

**George Day – August 26, 1972**

Maj George 'Bud' Day was awarded the Medal of Honor for his actions as a prisoner of war.

He had been shot down on August 26, 1967 while flying an F-100F on his 26th Fast FAC sortie, directing a flight of F-105s in an air strike against a SAM site. In the ejection, Day's right arm was broken in three places when he struck the side of the cockpit, and he also experienced eye and back injuries.

Day was unable to contact the rescue helicopter by survival radio and was quickly captured by North Vietnamese local militia. On his fifth night, when he was still within 20 miles of the DMZ, Day escaped from his initial captors despite his serious injuries. Although stripped of his boots and flight suit, Day crossed the DMZ back into South Vietnam, becoming the only US prisoner of war to escape from North Vietnam.

Within two miles of the US Marine base at Con Thien (and after 12-15 days of evading) he was captured again, this time by a Viet Cong patrol that wounded him in the leg and hand with gunfire. Taken back to his original camp, Day was tortured for escaping, breaking his right arm again. He then was moved to several prison camps near Hanoi, where he was periodically beaten, starved, and tortured.

On March 14, 1973, Day was released after five years and seven months as a North Vietnamese prisoner. On March 4, 1976, President Gerald Ford awarded Day the Medal of Honor for his personal bravery.

A North Vietnamese photo showing the wreckage of a B-52 in a lake in Hanoi. The wreckage is still there today

Capt Dick Myers (left) with his EWO Capt Don Triplett. The pair flew *Linebacker* missions over North Vietnam and Myers later rose to the rank of four-star general. From 2001-2005 he was the Chairman of the Joint Chiefs of Staff *(USAF Museum)*

B-52Ds from the Strategic Air Command line up for take-off as they prepare for strikes over Hanoi and Haiphong, North Vietnam *(USAF Museum)*

However, it proved impossible to throw the invading North Vietnamese divisions back over the border. Instead, as the fighting slackened, they established themselves in the countryside and waited for the Americans to return home.

### On-going Vietnamisation

Despite the intense fighting the Vietnamisation programme continued. The last USAF C-123 Provider squadron transferred its aircraft to the VNAF in June and Project *Enhance Plus* began in September with the aim of building up the VNAF to an adequate level to conduct operations, after the remaining USAF aircraft and 43,000 advisers and administrative troops left the country. By November, 288 more aircraft had been supplied to South Vietnam, comprising 116 F-5s, 90 A-37s, 28 A-1s, 22 AC-119Ks and 32 C-130As. As the *Linebacker I* campaign continued, the *Constant Guard* series of deployments recommenced with the arrival of two F-111A squadrons (the 428th and 430th TFS) at Takhli on September 28.

Three squadrons of A-7D Corsairs from the 354th TFW began to arrive at Korat in October – the first appearance of USAF A-7s in Southeast Asia. They replaced the F-4Es of *Constant Guard II* and flew their first combat missions on October 16. Three weeks later they were given the additional task of replacing the Skyraider in the Sandy escort role for the SAR helicopters.

### "Peace is at Hand"

In the meantime, North Vietnamese negotiators in Paris convinced Nixon's National Security Advisor, Henry Kissinger's negotiating team that they were willing seriously to discuss peace. As a result, all bombing was halted above the 20th Parallel again on October 23 and Kissinger confidently announced that 'Peace is at hand'. He should have known better…

During November the last US air bases in Vietnam were transferred to the VNAF. Now all combat missions would have to be flown from bases in Thailand. Meanwhile, the North Vietnamese took advantage of the bombing halt to repair the damage done over the preceding six months. The

**Feet wet. A USAF HH-3E rescues a pilot from the water off the coast of Vietnam** *(USAF Museum)*

**An RA-5C Vigilante from the USS *Ranger* cruises back after a mission over North Vietnam** *(US Navy)*

**Aerial refuelling permitted tactical aircraft to operate in the northern part of North Vietnam** *(USAF Museum)*

main lines of communication, particularly the railroads from China, were soon serviceable and newly-arrived supplies began to flow south again. By mid-December more MiG-21s had arrived at Gia Lam airfield, the monsoon season was approaching and the talks in Paris were getting nowhere.

The peace talks finally collapsed on December 13, by which time President Nixon had had enough. He had been re-elected for a second term in November and with domestic problems mounting, he wanted the war finished and the POWs returned. It was time to send the North Vietnamese a message that they would clearly understand, and that meant B-52 attacks.

## Destination Hanoi

At 14.51hrs local time, on December 18 1972, Maj Bill Stocker's black-bellied B-52D *Rose 1* slowly lumbered onto the end of the runway at Andersen AFB on Guam. Smoke spewed from the engines it slowly accelerated into the air, followed by 86 other BUFFs. Their destination was Hanoi.

The decision to launch Operation *Linebacker II* had been taken by President Nixon a few days earlier when he told Admiral Thomas Moorer, the Chairman of the Joint Chiefs of Staff, 'This is your chance to use military power to win this war'.

The restrictions were now lifted and the 155 B-52s on Guam (and 50 more at U Tapao in Thailand) were being given the chance to achieve what seven years of war had failed to so; to bring Hanoi to its knees by the swift, massive application of airpower against the heart of North Vietnam.

As the 87 B-52s from Guam and 42 more from Thailand neared Hanoi, the support forces began to play their part. Specially configured F-4s laid down chaff while EB-66s, EA-3s and EA-6s with ECM equipment helped to create additional clutter on the enemy radar screens and further hide the bombers. Navy fighter-bombers attacked coastal gun emplacements and SAM sites while USAF F-4s, F-111s and A-7s attacked airfields and SAM sites along the B-52 ingress

A Cessna A-37A of the 8th Tactical Fighter Wing over Vietnam in September 1972 *(USAF Museum)*

and egress routes. F-105 *Wild Weasels* searched for enemy radar signals, against which they would launch their Shrike radar homing missiles. EC-121s provided early warning of any threat by North Vietnamese fighters to the Phantoms flying Combat Air Patrol and, out in the Gulf, search and rescue helicopters waited to provide recovery help, if required.

An F-4C *Wild Weasel* flying over North Vietnam in December 1972. Unlike the F-105G, the F-4C Wild Weasel could not carry standard missiles *(USAF Museum)*

## *Linebacker II*

The 129 bombers arrived in three waves, four to five hours apart and attacked the airfields at Hoa Lac, Kep and Phuc Yen, the Kinh No complex and the Yen Vien railyards.

Captain Hal Wilson in the lead B-52 from U Tapao reported "Wall to wall SAMs up ahead" as he neared the outskirts of Hanoi. Shortly afterwards his B-52D was hit by a SAM missile and destroyed, along with two other G models from Andersen. Despite the 200 SAMs fired at the attackers, 94% of the bombs were on target and one MiG that got too close was shot down by a tail gunner. By the time the strike force had returned to Guam, the B-52s participating in the next day's raid were preparing to depart.

On December 19 all three waves of bombers hit their targets and although some were damaged, none were shot down. That all changed a day later when 99 bombers (in three waves) were met by 220 SAMs. Six B-52s were shot down – which was hardly surprising because the bombers used the same routes and tactics each day. It was even reported that some MiGs were flying alongside the bombers and relaying their altitude and heading to the SAM sites on the ground.

The following day, the bombers approached and departed along six different tracks over the Gulf and their missions were completed without loss.

On December 23, the US bombers made random changes in altitude and heading following bomb release and all aircraft returned safely. Similar tactics were used on Christmas Eve, when they attacked the Thai Nguyen and Kep railyards and – for the third day running – no aircraft was lost, but another MiG went down to a B-51 tail gunner.

The American bomber force had a well-deserved rest during the 24-hour Christmas Day ceasefire but on Boxing Day the most ambitious raid to date took place when 120 bombers in ten waves struck ten different targets around Hanoi and Haiphong. In order to saturate the enemy defences all bombing would be completed within 15 minutes, with all aircraft varying their altitudes, ingress and egress routes to avoid the many SAMs directed at the bomber force. Out of the 113 support aircraft and 120 bombers, only two did not make it back: *Ebony 2 a B-52D* was hit and exploded in mid-air and a damaged B-52, Ash 1, crashed just short of the runway at U Tapao with only two survivors.

On the ground, the effect of the bombing raid was dramatic. In the 'Hanoi Hilton' the American prisoners of war cheered wildly when the walls shook and plaster fell from the ceilings as the columns of B-52s rolled in.

A similar raid took place on Hanoi on December 27, when 60 B-52s and 101 support aircraft attacked seven targets releasing all their bombs in a mere 10 minutes. More SAMs were fired than the night before, but their aim was noticeably

> "Kissinger confidently announced that 'Peace is at hand'. He should have known better…"

**F-4D Phantoms from the 435th Tactical Fighter Squadron high over Vietnam as they await their turn to refuel** *(USAF Museum)*

**F-4Cs and F-4Ds did not have an internal gun but some were equipped with an external gun pod. Here, armourers load 20mm cannon rounds into a pod while other, complete, pods can be seen on the right** *(USAF Museum)*

poorer. One B-52 was shot down over Hanoi and another made it back over the border to Thailand before its crew was forced to bail out.

## Damage assessment

At last the weather had improved and the first bomb damage assessment photographs were obtained by *Olympic Torch* U-2R and *Giant Scale* SR-71 aircraft, together with drones launched by DC-130 *Buffalo Hunter* aircraft. The photographs showed that most of the bombers had been right on target, although one had missed Bach Mai airfield by 1,000 yards and had destroyed a wing of the nearby hospital.

The raids continued until December 30 when there were no more worthwhile targets left in the immediate Hanoi or Haiphong areas. The '11-Day War' had achieved its aim; the North Vietnamese wanted to talk again and serious negotiations began on January 8, 1973. At last, through the application of its air power the United States now held the upper hand.

The US position was accurately stated by Sir Robert Thompson, a recognised expert in counter-insurgency warfare and head of the British Advisory Mission to Vietnam from 1961 to 1965: "In my view, on 30 December 1972, after eleven days of those B-52 attacks on the Hanoi area, you had won the war. It was all over!" he said. "They had fired 1,242 SAMs, they had none left, and what would come in over land from China would be a mere trickle. They and their whole rear base at that point were at your mercy. They would have taken any terms. And that is why, of course, you actually got a peace agreement in January, which you had not been able to get in October."

Unfortunately, the USA failed to press home its advantage and demand more favourable terms, such as the withdrawal of all enemy troops from South Vietnam. This was mainly due to the clamour of the American public against President Nixon's offensive stand. They wanted an end to the war and the POWs brought home.

American prisoners of war cheer as their C-141 Starlifter takes off from Hanoi to ferry them home

# OPERATION *HOMECOMING*

**With the peace agreement signed, work began to bring home the US troops, prisoners and hardware. But the war in Laos and Cambodia continued to rage**

A peace agreement was finally signed on January 27, 1973 although South Vietnam's President Thieu was initially reluctant to sign it. He had good reason though; there were still 293,000 enemy troops in his country.

President Nixon advised Thieu that if he signed, he (Nixon) would intercede more vigorously with Congress for continued aid to South Vietnam and pledged to act forcefully towards any serious ceasefire violation by the North.

On the other hand, if Thieu did not sign, the United States would cut off all aid to South Vietnam. Needless to say, President Thieu agreed to sign.

## Operation *Endsweep*

On February 12, Operation *Homecoming* began and the first 116 prisoners of war were released in Hanoi. By March 29 the last of the 591 POWs had returned home to an ecstatic welcome.

At the same time Operation *Endsweep* began on February 27, when Navy CH-53 helicopters from Mine Countermeasures Squadron HM-12 started to clear the mines from Haiphong Harbour. It took until July 27 before the last mines were cleared from North Vietnamese waters.

Although the ceasefire agreement brought a halt to air operations over North and South Vietnam, the war still continued in Laos. During January 1973 US aircraft joined the Royal Lao Air Force in flying a total of 8,000 sorties against the North Vietnamese and Pathet Lao troops.

Finally the Pathet Lao and government forces agreed to a ceasefire on February 22 and all US tactical air support ceased on that day. Sporadic enemy violations of the ceasefire led to additional B-52 strikes in February and April, but the bombing finally ceased on April 17.

It took the Pathet Lao a further two and a half years to gain complete control of Laos and the King abdicated in December 1975, ending a 600 year-old monarchy. The People's Democratic Republic of Laos was proclaimed and the government's 185 US advisers were then replaced with 1,500 Soviet technicians.

Operation *Scoot* (Support Cambodia Out of Thailand) began in April to supply the Cambodian Government with food and ammunition. The North Vietnamese and Khmer Rouge forces were closing in on Phnom Penh so B-52s, F-111As, A-7s and AC-130s began to fly missions against enemy targets on the outskirts of the city.

## Watergate

However, the most crucial development relative to the situation in Vietnam during 1973 took place in the USA.

The Senate Watergate Committee was convened to investigate the infamous scandal after it was learned that 'Watergate burglars' had been directed to break into and wiretap the headquarters of the Democratic National Committee by President Richard Nixon's re-election campaign fund raising organisation – the Committee to Re-elect the President (CREEP). The Nixon administration had begun an irrevocable downward slide and Congress passed the Case-Church

> "By March 29 the last of the 591 POWs had returned home"

**Seen arriving at the National Museum of the United States Air Force on May 6, 2006 for permanent display, Lockheed C-141 Starlifter 'Hanoi Taxi' was the first aircraft to return Vietnam prisoners of war to the USA on February 12, 1973** *(USAF Museum)*

**By the end of 1973, the South Vietnamese Air Force was on its own and possessed a total of 2,075 aircraft including this Northrop F-5E Tiger II and Douglas Skyraider seen at Da Nang towards the end of that year** *(USAF Museum)*

**Some POWs didn't have to wait until 1973 to be freed – here injured USAF Capt David Baker awaits release at Loc Ninh in 1970** *(USAF Museum)*

Amendment ordering that no more funds were to be used to support directly, or indirectly, combat activities in or over Cambodia, Laos, North or South Vietnam by American forces after August 15.

## Short-lived peace

Of course, the communists had no intention of honouring the peace agreement. Soon Hanoi began to re-equip and reinforce its units in the South, including deploying 20 more anti-aircraft regiments complete with radar and SA-7 shoulder-fired missiles. These weapons afforded a degree of control over the country's airspace such that the Vietnamese Air Force could no longer operate over some areas. Under this ever-increasing anti-aircraft umbrella the communists began a 'land and population grab' campaign.

Regardless, US Congress passed the War Powers Resolution on October 12, 1973, which severely limited the President's traditional freedom of action regarding the employment of the armed forces. It was now virtually impossible for President Nixon to enforce the terms of the peace agreement or the guarantee given to President Thieu.

The South Vietnamese Air Force was now on its own. By the end of 1973, it possessed a total of 2,075 aircraft and had flown 458,000 sorties throughout the year. These had resulted in the loss of 185 aircraft, including 81 UH-1s, 26 O-1 Bird Dogs and 22 A-37s. ❖

**The processing delegation in Hanoi included military representatives from the USA and North Vietnam** *(USAF Museum)*

# THE AGE OF AUSTERITY

**With the promised US aid package slashed, the South Vietnamese Air Force was forced to mothball aircraft, reducing its capability to defend itself from the North**

The new year began with yet more student protests, but this time it was the US Embassy in Thailand that was the centre of attention. Together with recent changes in government, this marked the beginning of the end of the US military presence in the country and by August all USAF flying units had left Ubon and Takhli was returned to the Thai government in September.

Across the border in Cambodia, the improvement programme for the Khmer Air Force (KAF), known as Project *Flycatcher*, was terminated on June 30 after the transfer of 23 T-28D Trojans and a smaller number of C-47 Dakotas and Cessna O-1s had significantly improved the combat capability of the KAF.

**The improvement programme for the Cambodian Khmer Air Force, known as Project *Flycatcher*, was terminated on June 30 after the transfer of 23 T-28D Trojans** *(USAF Museum)*

## Cutting aid

The fate of South Vietnam was effectively sealed from July onwards when the US Congress began to cut back the amount of military aid to the Thieu government.

The original request for aid worth $1,600 million was eventually reduced to $700 million and austerity measures were introduced as a result. Over 200 Vietnamese Air Force (VNAF) aircraft were retired to flyable storage, including all the Skyraiders, O-1 observation aircraft and C-7, C-47 and C-119 transports. The 36 F-5E Tiger IIs, which the VNAF had only received in March, were also returned to the USA.

Troop reinforcement, resupply and medical evacuation were all seriously affected as the heli-lift capability was reduced by 70%. The airlift capability was also cut by 50% and the 32 VNAF C-130As were suffering from fuel leaks, wing cracks and spare parts shortages. As such between just four and eight Hercules were serviceable daily.

Naval activities were also reduced by 50%; river activities by 72%, and stocks of fuel and ammunition began to run down. In the meantime, enemy-initiated actions had increased by 70% over the previous year.

**Tensions in Thailand led to the beginning of the end of the US military presence in the country. By August all USAF flying units had left Ubon and Takhli was returned to the Thai government in September. Here, a USAF F-4 lines up alongside a Royal Thai Air Force T-28 Trojan at Ubon** *(USAF Museum)*

**The South Vietnamese government's original request for US aid worth $1,600 million was eventually reduced to $700 million and the resulting austerity measures resulted in many aircraft being retired to flyable storage, including all the remaining Skyraiders** *(USAF Museum)*

## Changing the guard

To add to South Vietnam's troubles, President Nixon resigned on August 9 and Vice-President Gerald Ford became the 38th President of the United States. South Vietnam now watched the run-down of USAF units in Thailand as America turned its back on the war.

The war had cost America dear; 58,000 service members had died and the cost alone of the 3,720 aircraft and 4,868 helicopters lost to all causes came to almost $7 billion. Now US aid had been drastically cut and South Vietnam had to deal with a hostile Congress and a new President.

The VNAF had lost 299 aircraft during 1974 and its strength was now down to 1,484, with fuel and ammunition stocks for only two months of operations. They awaited the forthcoming North Vietnamese offensive with trepidation.

The end came on December 13, when the enemy went on the offensive in Phuoc Long Province. Although the province was not of strategic importance, the loss of the first provincial capital in South Vietnam came as a shock to the population and armed forces. The victory was also of great psychological and political significance to the North Vietnamese. There had been no reaction, let alone punishment by the United States; what more encouragement could the communists have asked for?

North Vietnam already had 13 divisions in the South on the eve of the final offensive and a reserve of seven in the North. Russia and China had provided the enemy with enough supplies for a 15 to 20-month campaign.

Many VNAF Hueys flew out to the US Seventh Fleet but were forced to ditch in the sea due to overcrowded decks

# EVACUATION

**With the North Vietnamese rapidly overrunning the South, the VNAF put up a brave fight; but it was soon time to evacuate the country**

Late in 1974, the South Vietnamese Vice-President, Tran Van Huong, had insisted on replacing General Nguyen Van Toan, the very competent commander of II Corps, because of charges of corruption. His replacement by Major General Pham Van Phu was to contribute to the rapid disintegration of the South Vietnamese armed forces in 1975.

In January, the II Corps intelligence officers warned the new commander that the North Vietnamese were preparing to attack the city of Ban Me Thuot. However, General Phu disagreed and the bulk of his forces were in the Pleiku area when the attack on Ban Me Thuot began on March 9, 1975.

A very heavy artillery bombardment hit the city, followed by a tank and infantry assault and within 24 hours half the city and both airfields were lost. Despite President Thieu's order to the Army of the Republic of Vietnam (ARVN) 23rd Division to hold the city at all costs and 200 close air support sorties flown by the Vietnamese Air Force (VNAF), the city was in enemy hands by March 14.

Hueys were pushed overboard to make additional space for refugees desperate to land

US Marines provide cover during Operation *Eagle Pull* as Americans and Cambodians board Marine helicopters in Phnom Penh during the final US pullout of Cambodia *(US Navy)*

## Ignoring the VNAF

The same day that Ban Me Thuot fell, President Thieu held a strategic planning meeting at Cam Ranh Bay. The VNAF was not represented, although its airpower was the only means of offsetting the advantage that the North Vietnamese possessed in numbers and firepower.

Thieu ordered General Phu to withdraw his forces from Pleiku and Kontum and move them 160 miles southeast to Nha Trang in order to shorten the lines of defence in Military Region II and provide forces for a counter attack against the strategically important Ban Me Thuot. Instead of carefully organising a gradual withdrawal, Phu ordered a hasty pull-out, which cost II Corps the loss of 75% of its strength within ten days.

The VNAF's 6th Air Division was given 48 hours to evacuate all its aircraft and personnel from Pleiku to Phu Cat and Phan Rang. Although General Vinh, the commander of the VNAF, had not been forewarned about the withdrawal, he sent some C-130s to assist with the move. There was not enough time to ready all the stored aircraft for departure and 64 were left behind, including 21 A-1s, 11 O-2s and four O-1s.

## Refugee rout

As news of the military withdrawal reached the civilian population of Pleiku, a mass exodus began and troops and refugees streamed towards Tuy Hoa. Indiscriminate enemy artillery fire, ambushes and roadblocks turned the retreat into a rout, with the survivors reaching Tuy Hoa on March 28.

Communist troops took over Pleiku and Kontum without a fight and Ban Me Thuot would not be recaptured because II Corps no longer had any combat troops. Air America assisted in the evacuation of Pleiku; one of its 51-seat Curtiss C-46 Commandos flew out with 142 troops on board and took 90 miles to climb to 1,000ft.

Within days, the communists were in control of the whole of Quang Tri Province and the tired remnants of I Corps' divisions were gathered in three enclaves along the coast at Hue, Da Nang and Chu Lai. The three cities proved indefensible and Hue was abandoned on the night of March 25 and Chu Lai a day later. The badly organised withdrawal from Hue was disrupted by enemy fire and any discipline remaining among the soldiers of the 1st Infantry Division soon vanished. Only a third of the troops reached Da Nang and these quickly disappeared in search of their families and a way out.

> "A USAF C-5 Galaxy transport aircraft carrying orphans from Saigon crashed"

**Operation *Babylift* was marred by the loss of a Galaxy on April 4. The cargo doors blew out and damaged the tail and control cables with the resulting crash landing killed many of the children and adults on board**

The first US Marine Corpos CH-53 Sea Stallions arrive at the US Embassy compound in Saigon on April 29, 1975. They had launched from the USS *Hancock* and over the next 18 hours helicopters evacuated nearly 9,000 Americans, Vietnamese and foreign nationals from the city *(US Navy)*

## Evacuation

The defences at Da Nang soon caved in and during the morning of March 29 some 10,000 defenders were evacuated by sea. The 1st Air Division managed to fly out 130 aircraft but 180 more and most of the division's personnel were left behind.

Since the start of the offensive, over half a million refugees had converged on Da Nang and when the enemy began to shell the city, panic set in. Any aircraft landing at the airbase was mobbed by hundreds of Vietnamese and it finally became so unsafe that the airlift was suspended.

The President of World Airways, Ed Daly, took the last evacuation flight into Da Nang, but instead of picking up refugees, 270 American soldiers from the Black Panthers, one of the Army's toughest units, fought their way onto the plane. A frustrated soldier outside threw a grenade at the wing and the explosion jammed the flaps open and the undercarriage down. Four soldiers rode in the wheel wells to Saigon, but one fell to his death on the way.

General Frederick C Weyand, the US Army Chief of Staff arrived in Saigon to meet the US Ambassador and President Thieu. General Cao Van Vien, the chairman of the South Vietnamese Joint General Staff, asked the American delegation if B-52s could be used to bomb enemy troop concentrations. The answer was negative.

With 325,000 enemy troops advancing southward, some heroic fights were put up by small ARVN units. Elsewhere, the 6th Air Division which had withdrawn from Pleiku to Phu Cat and Phan Rang eventually put up the best fight of the war. Its Cessna A-37s flew an all-out effort with some pilots loading their own aircraft as ground crew fought as infantrymen after the ARVN pulled out. Eventually Phan Rang was overrun on April 16.

## Operation *Babylift*

Operation *Babylift* was the name given to the mass evacuation of 3,300 children from South Vietnam to the USA and other countries (including Australia, France, and Canada) between April 3–26, 1975. Along with Operation *New Life*, over 110,000 refugees were evacuated from the country and thousands of children were adopted by families around the world.

> "One fleeing F-5 even carried two pilots instead of the usual one!"

Sadly, tragedy would strike the programme on April 4 when a USAF C-5 Galaxy transport aircraft carrying orphans from Saigon crashed less than a mile from Tan Son Nhut airport. The cargo door had blown out shortly after take-off and the rudder and elevator control cables had jammed. The ensuing crash killed many of the orphans and their escorts.

Elsewhere, the war was also coming to an end in Cambodia. The communist forces had cut off the capital, Phnom Penh, from external resupply and had been laying siege to the city since January. President Lon Nol left the country on April 1 and with the final collapse imminent the US Embassy began evacuating its staff. Operation *Eagle Pull* began at dawn on April 12 when the first of eight Marine CH-53 helicopters landed in a football field and began to load 82 Americans, 159 Cambodians and 35 foreign nationals.

It would be two and a half hours before the last helicopter took off, just as a rocket exploded in the field. Before it was out of range, the CH-53 took a hit in its tail rotor from a 12.7mm machine gun, but the badly vibrating machine made it safely to Ubon. Five days later the city fell and Cambodia began to slide slowly back into the dark ages.

## Desperate defence

Meanwhile, back in South Vietnam the VNAF continued to fly around 180 sorties each day, mostly against defensive positions instead of the enemy convoys now moving bumper to bumper down coastal Highway One.

More than 150 bombing sorties were even flown by C-130s. From an altitude of 15-20,000ft, they dropped pallets loaded with three or four bombs. On nine occasions 15,000lb *Daisy Cutter* bombs were dropped from the Hercules. When the first one fell on enemy positions some four miles from Xuan Loc, the entire city shook as if rocked by an earthquake and all the lights went out. The explosion destroyed the headquarters of the NVA 341st Division and rumours began to spread that the B-52s had returned.

The last-ditch effort to defend Saigon took place east of the city at Xuan Loc between April 9 and 22. If Xuan Loc was overrun, the airfield, depot and arsenal at Bien Hoa would follow and, in an attempt to prevent this, the VNAF flew 600 sorties in support of the defenders.

However, on April 23 the ARVN 18th Division, together with the 1st Airborne Brigade, carried out an orderly retreat from the city. As the enemy flanked Xuan Loc and came within artillery range of Bien Hoa air base, all operational aircraft were flown out to Tan Son Nhut and Binh Thuy. For all practical purposes the war was over with the loss of Xuan Loc, although the VNAF still had 976 operational aircraft, including 92 A-37s and 93 F-5s.

## MEDAL OF HONOR

**Rear Admiral James Stockdale – March 4, 1976**

On March 4, 1976 Rear Admiral James Stockdale became the last person to receive the Medal of Honor for actions during the Vietnam War [although a few others were later backdated when regulations changed].

Stockdale was privy to one of the most closely guarded secrets of the Vietnam War; what really happened in the Gulf of Tonkin on August 2, 1964 when the USS *Maddox* had been 'attacked.'

While flying an A-4E Skyhawk from the USS *Oriskany* on September 9, 1965, Stockdale was struck by enemy fire and ejected. He parachuted into a small village, where he was severely beaten and taken prisoner. He was held as a prisoner of war in the Hoa Lo prison for the next seven and a half years and lived in fear that he would be forced to reveal his secret about the *Maddox*.

Stockdale was one of eleven prisoners known as the 'Alcatraz Gang' due to his resistance but was released from captivity in 1973. On March 4, 1976, Stockdale was awarded the Medal of Honor by President Gerald Ford for his conduct as a prisoner of war. He passed away in July 2005 aged 81.

# "The longest war in America's history came to an end"

## All-out

USAF C-130 Hercules and C-141 Starlifters began airlifting American and South Vietnamese refugees out of Tan Son Nhut airport on April 20. The following day, President Thieu resigned and transferred the presidency to Vice-President Tran Van Houng.

On April 28, five ex-VNAF A-37s (captured by pilots from the North) attacked the airport with 250lb bombs, destroying three VNAF AC-119s and several C-47s.

General Duong Van Minh was sworn in as President the same day, but he would not be in post for long; 15 enemy divisions now encircled Saigon and time was running out.

In the early hours of the April 29, Tan Son Nhut airport came under fire again and a USAF C-130 was destroyed on the ground. As the enemy artillery scored a direct hit on the main fuel depot, VNAF aircraft began to take-off and head for Thailand. At least 132 VNAF aircraft were flown to U Tapao in Thailand, including A-37s, A-1s, three AC-119s and at least two dozen F-5s – one of which carried two pilots instead of the usual one!

A handful of VNAF pilots fought to the end and one AC-119 which had been patrolling the perimeter of Tan Son Nhut all night landed to refuel and rearm and took off again just before daybreak. At 07.00hrs, the gunship was hit by an SA-7 missile and plunged to the ground in flames.

## Operation *Frequent Wind*

With the runway at Tan Son Nhut now closed by enemy fire, US Ambassador Graham Martin gave the order to evacuate all US personnel from Saigon on April 29. It was not a moment too soon and that afternoon the first Marine CH-53s and H-46s arrived, together with USAF HH-52Bs flown off the USS *Midway*. Over the next 18 hours these helicopters, together with Air America UH-1s, evacuated nearly 9,000 Americans, Vietnamese and foreign nationals. Of these, nearly 2,100 were lifted from the US Embassy compound alone.

Out in the South China Sea, the US Seventh Fleet waited as over 50 VNAF UH-1s and CH-47s brought out more refugees. Even an O-1 Bird Dog appeared with the pilot's family on board and made a successful landing on the USS *Midway*. Many UH-1s landed on the command ship *Blue Ridge* and were then pushed overboard to make room for others desperate to land.

At 07.30hrs on April 30, 1975, the eleven Marine guards who had been beating back the crowds of Vietnamese at the US Embassy in Saigon, made a dash for the roof of the building. At the top of the stairs they turned and threw tear-gas grenades behind them and then climbed aboard a waiting Marine CH-53. The ramp came up and the helicopter lifted off.

At 10.00hrs that morning the government of South Vietnam surrendered and the longest war in America's history came to an end. ❖

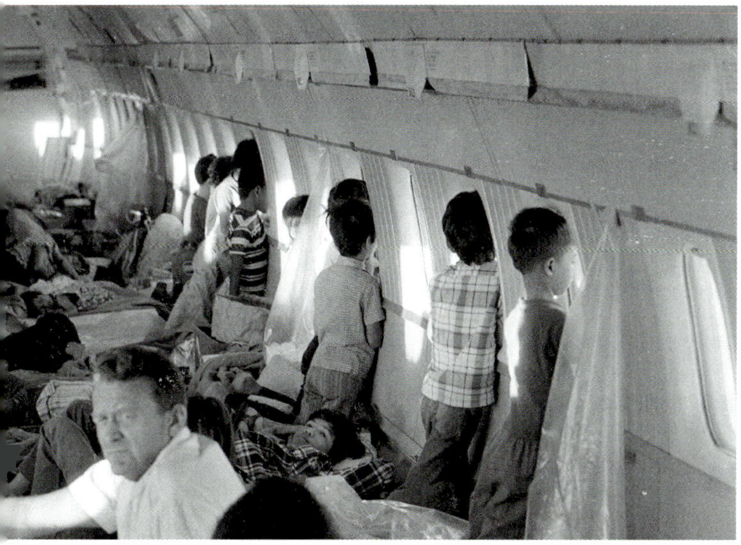

**Operation *Babylift* involved the evacuation of 2,000 South Vietnamese displaced children – most of which were flown to America. Here, the first load of 'passengers' admire the view from the windows of the C-141 Starlifter transport aircraft** *(USAF Museum)*

**Victorious North Vietnamese troops run across the parking ramp at Saigons Tan Son Nhut air base as VNAF C-47s burn in the background**

# COUNTING THE COST

## The Vietnam War officially lasted 19 years, 5 months, 4 weeks and 1 day (from November 1, 1955 until April 30, 1975) and is estimated to have resulted in the deaths of more than 3,880,000 people

### CASUALTIES AND LOSSES (SOUTH & ALLIES)

| | |
|---|---|
| South Vietnam | Between 220,357 and 313,000 military dead<br>Around 1,170,000 wounded |
| United States | 58,307 dead (around 1,200 never found)<br>303,644 wounded<br>1,350 Missing in Action (MIA) |
| Australia | 500 dead<br>3,129 wounded |
| New Zealand | 37 dead<br>187 wounded |
| Philippines | 9 dead<br>64 wounded |
| South Korea | 5,099 dead<br>10,962 wounded<br>4 missing |
| Thailand | 351 dead<br>1,358 wounded |
| Total dead | Between 284,660 and 377,303 |
| Total wounded | Around 1,490,000 |

### CASUALTIES AND LOSSES (NORTH)

| | |
|---|---|
| North Vietnam/Viet Cong | Between 444,000 and 1,100,000 military dead / MIA<br>Around 600,000 wounded |
| China | Around 1,100 dead<br>Around 4,200 wounded |
| North Korea | 14 dead |
| Soviet Union | 16 dead |
| Total dead | Between 455,476 and 1,170,476 |
| Total wounded | Around 608,200 |

### CIVILIAN CASUALTIES AND LOSSES

| | |
|---|---|
| South Vietnamese civilian dead | Between 627,000 and 2,000,000 |
| Cambodian civilian dead | Between 200,000 and 300,000 |
| Laotian civilian dead | Between 20,000 and 200,000 |
| Total civilian dead | Between 912,000 and 2,500,000 |

### AIRCRAFT LOSSES

| Royal Australian Air Force | |
|---|---|
| Bell UH-1 Iroquois | 6 |
| DHC C-7 Caribou | 3 |
| English Electric Canberra | 2 |
| CAC Sabre | 2 |

| North Vietnamese People's Air Force* | |
|---|---|
| Antonov An-2 *Colt* | 2 |
| Mikoyan-Gurevitch MiG-17 *Fresco* | 100 |
| Mikoyan-Gurevitch MiG-19 *Farmer* | 10 |
| Mikoyan-Gurevitch MiG-21 *Fishbed* | 86 |

| People's Republic of China Air Force | |
|---|---|
| Mikoyan-Gurevitch MiG-17 Fresco | 1 |

| South Vietnam Air Force | |
|---|---|
| All aircraft types* | 72 ** |

| USAF (Fixed Wing) | |
|---|---|
| Beechcraft QU-22 Pave Eagle | 8 |
| Boeing B-52 Stratofortress | 31 |
| Boeing KB-50 Superfortress | 1 |
| Boeing KC-135 Stratotanker | 3 |
| Cessna A-37 Dragonfly | 22 |
| Cessna O-1 Bird Dog | 172 |
| Cessna O-2 Skymaster | 104 |
| Cessna U-3B Blue Canoe | 1 |
| Convair F-102 Delta Dagger | 14 |
| DHC C-7 Caribou | 19 |
| DHC U-6A Beaver | 1 |
| Douglas A-1 Skyraider | 191 |
| Douglas A-26 Invader | 22 |
| Douglas AC-47 Spooky | 19 |
| Douglas C-47 Skytrain | 21 |
| Douglas E/RB-66 Destroyer | 14 |
| Fairchild AC-119 Shadow | 6 |
| Fairchild C-123 Provider | 53 |
| General Dynamics F-111A Aardvark | 11 |
| Grumman HU-16 Albatross | 4 |
| Helio U-10 Courier | 1 |
| Lockheed AC-130 Spectre | 6 |
| Lockheed C-5A Galaxy | 1 |
| Lockheed C-141 Starlifter | 2 |
| Lockheed EC-121 BatCat | 2 |
| Lockheed F-104 Starfighter | 14 |
| Lockheed SR-71 Blackbird | 2 |
| Lockheed U-2 'Dragon Lady' | 1 |
| Martin B-57 Canberra | 56 |
| McDonnell RF-101 Voodoo | 39 |
| McDonnell Douglas F-4 Phantom II | 445 |
| McDonnell Douglas RF-4 Phantom II | 83 |
| North American F-100 Super Sabre | 243 |
| North American T-28 Trojan | 23 |
| Northrop F-5 Freedom Fighter | 9 |
| Republic F-105 Thunderchief | 382 |
| Rockwell OV-10 Bronco | 63 |
| Vought/LTV A-7D Corsair II | 6 |

| USAF (Rotary Wing) | |
|---|---|
| Bell UH-1 Iroquois | 36 |
| Kaman HH-43B Huskie/Pedro | 13 |
| Sikorsky CH/HH-3 Jolly Green Giant | 34 |
| Sikorsky CH/HH-53 Super Jolly | 27 |

| US Navy (Fixed Wing) | |
|---|---|
| Douglas A-1/EA-1 Skyraider | 69 |
| Douglas A-3/KA-3 Skywarrior | 9 |
| Douglas A-4 Skyhawk | 282 |
| Douglas C-47 Skytrain | 1 |
| Grumman A-6 Intruder | 62 |
| Grumman C-1 Trader | 4 |
| Grumman C-2 Greyhound | 1 |
| Grumman E-1 Tracer | 3 |
| Grumman E-2 Hawkeye | 2 |
| Grumman S-2 Tracker | 5 |
| Lockheed P-2 Neptune | 4 |
| Lockheed P-3 Orion | 2 |
| McDonnell Douglas F-4 Phantom II | 138 |
| North American RA-5 Vigilante | 27 |
| Rockwell OV-10 Bronco | 7 |
| Vought/LTV A-7 Corsair | 100 |
| Vought/LTV F-8 Crusader | 118 |
| Vought/LTV RF-8 Crusader | 29 |

| US Navy (Rotary Wing) | |
|---|---|
| Kaman SH-2/UH-2 Sea Sprite | 12 |
| Sikorsky SJ-3 Sea King | 20 |

| US Marine Corps (Fixed Wing) | |
|---|---|
| Cessna O-1 Bird Dog | 7 |
| Douglas A-4 Skyhawk | 81 |
| Douglas C-117 Skytrain | 2 |
| Douglas EF-10 Skynight | 5 |
| Grumman A-6/EA-6A Intruder | 27 |
| Douglas TA-4 Skyhawk | 10 |
| Grumman TF-8 Cougar | 1 |
| Lockheed KC-130 Hercules | 4 |
| McDonnell Douglas F-4 Phantom II | 95 |
| McDonnell Douglas R-4 Phantom II | 4 |
| Rockwell OV-10 Bronco | 10 |
| Vought/LTV F-8 Crusader | 21 |
| Vought/LTV RF-8 Crusader | 1 |

| US Marine Corps (Rotary Wing) | |
|---|---|
| Bell AH-1 Cobra | 7 |
| Bell UH-1E Huey | 69 |
| Boeing Vertol CH-46D Sea Knight | 109 |
| Sikorsky H-34/HUS-1 | 75 |
| Sikorsky CH-37 Mojave | 1 |
| Sikorsky CH-53 Sea Stallion | 9 |

| US Army (Fixed Wing) | |
|---|---|
| Cessna O-1 Bird Dog | 297 |
| Grumman OV-1 Mohawk | 67 |

| US Army (Rotary Wing) | |
|---|---|
| Bell AH-1 Cobra | 270 |
| Bell H-13 Sioux | 3 |
| Bell OH-58 Kiowa | 45 |
| Bell UH-1 Iroquois | 3,090 |
| Boeing CH-47 Chinook | 132 |
| Hiller OH-23 Raven | 93 |
| Hughes OH-6 Cayuse | 842 |
| Piasecki CH-21C Shawnee | 14 |
| Sikorsky CH-37 Mojave | 1 |
| Sikorsky CH-54 Tarhe | 9 |
| Sikorsky H-34 | 176 |

**Aircraft claimed by US and Allied pilots*
*** 72 VNAF aircraft were reported shot down – types unknown*

Among the countless memorials to the men and women who served during the Vietnam War this statue – dubbed 'The Three Servicemen' – in Washington DC is one of the most poignant. The US capital will also, eventually, be home to the Vietnam Veterans Memorial Center (VVMC); a high-tech facility commemorating the service and sacrifice of 2.7 million uniformed Americans who saw service in South East Asia. When completed the VVMC will become part of the National Park Service and be operated by the National Mall. To learn more visit www.buildthecenter.org *(Both Steve Bridgewater)*

This thought provoking wall of names can be found in downtown Philadelphia and is typical of the memorials in major cities throughout the USA